SAY ONE KIND THING

Editor: Rebecca Kaplan
Designer: Heesang Lee
Managing Editor: Glenn Ramirez
Production Manager: Rachael Marks

Library of Congress Control Number: 2022946058

ISBN: 978–1-4197–5755–6
eISBN: 978–1-64700–547–4

Some names and identifying characteristics have been changed. This book contains the experiences, opinions, and ideas of its author. It is intended to provide helpful and informative material on the subject addressed, and is sold with the understanding that the author and publisher are not engaged in rendering health, medical, or any other kind of personal or professional advice or services.

Abrams Image books are available at special discounts when purchased in quantity for premiums and promotions as well as fundraising or educational use. Special editions can also be created to specification. For details, contact specialsales@abramsbooks.com or the address below.

Abrams Image® is a registered trademark of Harry N. Abrams, Inc.

ABRAMS The Art of Books
195 Broadway, New York, NY 10007
abramsbooks.com

SAY ONE KIND THING

Lessons in Acceptance, Love, and Letting Go

SUSAN VERDE

ABRAMS IMAGE, NEW YORK

To my mom and dad, J and J.
Thank you for bringing me into this world
to experience, learn, love, and grow.
I am forever grateful.

PREFACE

As someone who writes books for children, the idea of writing for adults was exciting but also daunting, not just because the process is so different but also because I knew I would have to share more and let more of myself show. My books for kids are infused with mindfulness and ways to love yourself and take care of the world, so that was my intention for this book, but for the "big kids." It seemed that writing about my own evolution in the area of self-love might be a lovely way to give insight into my "why" for supporting children in this way. However, as I began writing, I found myself reopening old traumas and often overwhelmed with anxiety and insecurity. I quickly realized that if I was going to talk about my own inner critic and view of myself, I would need to be willing to be vulnerable and honest. I will admit that there were many times this stopped me in my tracks as I was writing, worrying about how much to share or what others might think. At a certain point though, I knew I either had to toss the book aside or lean in and let go, dropping my focus on a certain outcome and just being myself, whatever that meant. I chose the latter.

There was a lot to learn about myself as I wrote this book and a lot to relearn. One thing I know is that we all have trauma and suffering, and it looks different for everyone. I recognize that I was provided the resources and the ability to seek out support and find time for inner work and introspection. I know that is not everyone's experience and I don't take it for granted nor do I intend to suggest that my ways of coping and learning about myself and my relationships are how it *should* be done. There are no *shoulds* in this book. There is only me, sharing my experience openly, and a hope that you, the reader, will find yourself seen somewhere within these essays and that you will know you are not alone.

INTRODUCTION:

THE INNER DICTIONARY

In middle school, my father decided that my brother and I should improve our vocabularies. I am not entirely sure why he felt we weren't learning enough vocab words in school. But nonetheless, this was our task. He gave us each a brand-new dictionary, with crinkly thin, almost transparent pages and alphabetical indentations, and a file box full of blank index cards. We were instructed to look up a word each day, write it down with its definition on one of the cards, and create a sentence using the word. This was no different than the vocabulary lessons we had at school, but for doing this at home, we would each receive five dollars at the end of the week after he tested us on our word memorization.

My father had grown up with basically nothing. His family was one of a few Jewish families living in Tulsa, Oklahoma, and from a very young age, he dealt with the heaviness of an alcoholic mother and the absence of his father. Somehow, he did well in school and always found himself work. We often heard stories of his summer jobs picking peas for the pea harvest. Recognizing the world held more, he was determined to get out of there, to find a sense of self-worth and achieve something better. Being highly intelligent and hyper-focused, he managed to earn scholarships to go away to college and then business school, which led him to a career in finance. Here is where he felt successful and capable. In this world he thrived, savoring the approval of his peers and earning more than he had ever imagined was possible. Although this allowed our family a lot of privilege growing up, it was also a strange dynamic. He couldn't figure out his relationship with money. It seemed like he never felt deserving of it and was often stressed and concerned about losing it. He was not ostentatious or snobby, and in retrospect, I personally don't think he ever really fit in with the usual Wall Street crowd. He was known in his industry for his fairness and honesty, which appeared to be an anomaly in that world. But ultimately, money became how he measured himself and often how he tried to make sure we, his children, were "measuring up" as well.

So being offered a monetary reward in exchange for memorizing a few vocab words as a means of bettering ourselves was not surprising. And there were parts of this task that appealed to me beyond the five bucks. I loved feeling the weight of that giant dictionary, closing my eyes, flipping through pages to land on the most obscure and interesting words, and putting them into sentences. But this all lost its luster after about two weeks in. I had little trouble memorizing words and creating sentences. I knew that this pleased my father, which was the never-ending and never-fully-achieved goal of my existence. But ultimately, the memorizing and the pleasing and the five dollars weren't worth it to me. It became a meaningless and redundant exercise, as I realized random words chosen out of context were not ones I wanted to spend my time with. When I stopped, I expected disappointment from my father and it came. If I couldn't stick with this one activity, how would I ever be able to learn or achieve anything? Apparently, my whole life was ruined in one fell swoop. "And," my father added with irritation, "no money for you!"

It took me many years to understand what this dictionary game represented: a transactional relationship with my father where love was given in exchange for achievement. As I grew, this model would lead me to question my own value, time and again. What *was* I worth? Five dollars a week? Kindness? Consistency? Unconditional love? I wasn't sure.

And these random dictionary words he was telling us to learn didn't counter the vocabulary of his constant disappointment that he had handed down to us. The words I longed for were ones of love and comfort. Instead, over the years, I compiled my own inner dictionary of words that were self-critical and loud. With every subsequent failure or stumble or even achievement, I would open *that* dictionary, flipping through it in my head, landing on just the right word, and putting it into a sentence to capture my self-doubt, to criticize and berate myself. This was the dictionary of me. I held onto it, carrying it with me wherever I went.

When I was a child, there was a word my father said to me over and over again. He said it when he was disappointed in me, when he thought I had made a mistake or a poor choice, or when he was just plain angry.

Worthless.

At a young age, this word got caught in the fibers of my brain. This word got stuck in the muscles of my body. This word became the suitcase I carried with me into adulthood. It's the word that made me mistrust my achievements and the compliments I received. At any given moment, this was the word that would come at me like a punch in the gut, knocking the wind out of me.

Worthless.

At a certain point, my dad didn't have to say it anymore. It was something I could feel in his tone or see in his eyes. And eventually, I believed it to be so, and it became a word I said to myself. This was the mantra of my inner critic: *Worthless.* My successes weren't enough. I was not enough. And of course, the failures made sense; after all, I now understood this to be who I was at my core.

I remember wishing for an explanation from my father. Why was I worthless? How had he reached this conclusion about me? I wanted to know specifically what I had done or hadn't done. Or was I just born this way? I also wanted an apology and acknowledgment that he was wrong and really, I was worth everything! But those words never came.

Ultimately, as an adult, I would gain insight into why he spoke to me this way. The trauma he carried from his own childhood, the helplessness and fear and lack of his own self-worth were feelings he never resolved, and they leaked into *his* adult life. The frustrations, and pressures of being a father and a husband, and the chaos and unknowns of raising a family triggered the fear that was ever-present and filled him with anger and rage. Having had no healthy model for expressing his anger and fear, he lashed out. He was not the same person at work because that was an environment he could control. He knew how to do that. He felt safe and confident and capable. But home was a different story.

There were moments of calm and connection between us. Sometimes we had fun together. My father taught me to swim and took me to musicals and made a lot of jokes. Every so often, we spoke of feelings or things beneath the surface. He had a gentle, endearing way of calling me "Suz," and when he smiled it was big and bright. In those moments, I would feel he had the capacity to love me, and that he had loving words for me too, but they were always too quiet in my mind.

As I grew, so did my inner dictionary. More words came from family, school, the world. Although new, kinder words appeared, words like "worthless" were the ones that stuck. They always hit deeper and rang louder. I wondered if I would ever be able to shut them up. Words like:

Fat.

Lazy.

Weird.

Short.

Ugly.

Awkward.

Stupid.

The list went on . . .

This was my lexicon. I accepted these words as my truth, contributing to the very definition of me, *Susan*. Throughout my childhood and into adulthood, I was riddled with anxiety and fell into periods of deep depression. I didn't know how to love myself. I didn't even know I was *allowed* to love myself.

I searched desperately for outside approval. I had to be thin. I had to get good grades. I had to achieve. I gravitated toward friends who shared a similar inner monologue. We would connect over our imperfect bodies and perceived shortcomings. At the same time, I also found people who didn't operate this way, and I would feed off their self-confidence. I craved words that were positive, but even when I heard them, I couldn't internalize them. I didn't really believe they were true because my own inner critic was louder and every "mistake" I made was confirmation of the real, worthless me.

During one of my lowest points as a young adult, a friend who always seemed to have her sh*t together and was still for some reason hanging out with me took me to my first yoga class. I should say she practically dragged me there. I remember wearing super baggy clothes because I was ashamed of my body. I tried to use my lack of cute yoga attire to talk my way out of it. But my friend pleaded and asked that I try "Just once . . . give it a try just once."

The whole excursion was daunting but as we entered the studio there was a calming vibe with a smell of Palo Santo smudge sticks and lavender essential oil. As I timidly walked up to the counter to check in, those words in my head hit me hard. I was certain that through this experience I would be told

You are

Fat

Ugly
Unfit
Out of place
Worthless
You don't belong here.

But the beautiful soul behind the counter did not say any of these things. Instead, she smiled softly and said, "Welcome, so happy you are here."

That first class, I tucked myself in a corner and just tried to follow along. It was a difficult class and there were moments I just lay on my mat. But there were others around me doing the same. I wasn't out of place. I wasn't the "worst" in the class. I was thankfully anonymous. People were focusing on their own experiences, and ultimately, I was able to focus on mine. The gentle movement felt good in my body, but I was mostly struck by a new set of words coming from the teacher. To my surprise, these words didn't seem scripted but rather as if they were coming from that teacher's inner truth.

I am thankful you are all here
Showing up is enough
Do what feels good to you
It is your body
There is no right or wrong way
Every experience is OK
Let go

These phrases, spoken so naturally by the teacher, were enough to quiet my mind for that hour. At the end of class, we were all on our backs in savasana, and she asked us to place our hands on our bellies and to just notice that we were there in that moment . . . breathing. She showed us how to anchor our minds to our breath and how to bring our attention back to our breath when our minds wandered. In those last few moments of class, I felt a calmness and safety that was new to me.

I was struck by this feeling and by the new words that lingered in my brain once the class ended.

I wanted more, needed more, and I was eager to return. But there was also a part of me that didn't really trust these words or this new feeling, that wanted to see if the experience could be repeated.

I dragged myself to class after class. Hiding in corners. The poses and sequences were helping my body, but I was there for the words. I wanted to know if these thoughts, these words, were for real, or if this was yoga class–specific. Did people really speak and feel this way outside of a yoga studio—that everyone was worthy, and that self-love was achievable and important? I heard different teachers whose classes I took say many of the same things. Somehow, it never felt scripted, but rather, like a new way of living that was possible. When I couldn't make it to class or couldn't afford it, I practiced what I remembered on my own. Stillness and breathing and sitting with myself. Observing my thoughts and letting them pass instead of fighting them. Practicing those new words from class until they were a part of me. It was work and not always easy but eventually I began to have tools. I was cultivating a love of myself.

When I heard "fat," I countered with "I am grateful for the body that I have that allows me to do so much."

When I heard "ugly," I said, "I am beautiful and unique."

When I heard "stupid," I said, "I am smart enough to learn and have come this far."

When I heard "worthless," I told myself, "I am important, and I make a difference."

These became my new mantras and affirmations. It wasn't a cure-all, but it was a start. I began to see that loving myself was essential. I began to make choices that reflected my desire for self-care. I began to surround myself with people who also cared about themselves. I pulled away from my childhood ideas of perfectionism and from beating myself up as the norm. I began to unlearn what I had internalized from the words of my father. Over time, as I grew stronger and learned to trust my own inner voice, I began to engage more fully in my life. Instead of feeling angry and withdrawn, I became compassionate and curious.

Eventually, I became a mother. After struggling for a long time to get pregnant, I was fortunate enough to be able to try IVF, and I finally gave birth to twin boys. These two miracles, one bald and chubby, and the other skinny as a bird with a head full of dark hair and big brown eyes, were so small and fragile upon their arrival. Before I had time to get used to the idea of these little humans as my own, their sibling arrived. Another miracle. Showing up with no help from labs and petri dishes; a gift, born with tiny toes and a big personality. In those months of pregnancy, I would often place my hands on my giant belly and talk gently to my children, promising them that I would not speak to them the way I had been spoken to. They would not inherit my inner critic. Instead, the words they would hear from me would only be filled with love and support.

But I wasn't prepared for the feelings that came along with caring for three needy, squirmy babies. I had not fully grasped what a huge responsibility raising little humans would be. They were depending on me to NOT MESS IT UP. In this place of not knowing, not sleeping, not doing it all the way every book said it *should* be done, everything I had worked so hard to change about myself was brought right back to the surface. The insecurity and self-loathing, there they were again.

The words.

Which became sentences.

Statements.

Declarations of truth.

You are not capable.

You are doing this wrong.

How are you even a mother?

You are:

WORTHLESS

There it was . . .

It felt like those words were reentering my mind and body and defining me in this new role as a parent. In my foggy, sleep-deprived state, I told myself that even if this was *my* truth, I would never let them know. And I would never let it be theirs. I thought I could protect my children and teach them to nurture their inner lives, while neglecting my own. But my inner critic was once again so loud. Keeping my feelings about myself shoved down deep and separate from my parenting proved to be unsustainable, and I began to crumble . . .

When I felt overwhelmed by motherhood, had difficulty breastfeeding, made mistakes, neglected self-care because I was convinced it was selfish—I called myself *stupid* and *incapable* and *worthless*. I felt shame. Shame that my body wasn't in shape. Shame that motherhood didn't feel like a constant joy. Shame that I was struggling. Shame in my own self-talk.

I was trying my best to *say* positive things to my kids. Meanwhile, I was *showing* them the terrible things going on in my own mind. Even though I didn't say these terrible things out loud, my actions and my demeanor were a reflection of those words. I was neglecting myself, unable to see all that I was capable of and only focusing on how I might be failing and the things going wrong. Perhaps there was an element of postpartum at play, but I was not giving myself any attention. I let my interests, my looks, my practices take a back seat. I was showing these beautiful, brand-new humans right from the start that loving yourself isn't possible. I was letting my inner critic do the parenting and I knew this was rubbing off on my kids.

I recognized that I needed to return to the practices that had supported me in the past—the yoga, the meditation, the nurturing self-talk. I needed to make time for them again, or all my good intentions for my children would be lost, and I would be lost.

So, my practice began, again, slowly. At first, it was like being right back in that first yoga class, where just getting there had been a challenge, and everything felt fake and forced and exhausting. Parenting required so much of me and returning to my practice felt like one more item on my to-do list, a chore, more work. But I knew there was value in putting that time in because I had done it before. And this time, there would be no going to a class or sitting in the presence of a teacher. It was up to me alone. In the rare moments of quiet that I could find, I began to focus on intentional breathing and on speaking kindly to myself. I started by saying just one kind thing to myself—I remember it well:

You are doing the best you can and that is good enough.

That mantra was on repeat for a while until eventually I came to believe it, and then I added more.

You are loved.

You are safe.

You are loving.

I became a bit of a walking cliché and a big fan of Post-it notes and refrigerator affirmations. I stuck these little notes for myself everywhere I could, so that they were right there in front of my face and so that my "mom brain" could not miss them. The more I spoke these words to myself and internalized them, the more I found that I could authentically say them and show them to my children.

Slowly, things began to shift. I rediscovered my tools. I made mistakes. Lots of them. I wasn't always kind or calm. I had moments of sadness, anxiety, anger, and worry that still have not gone away even now that my kids are teens. But I stopped getting stuck in a false and damaging narrative about myself. I wasn't worthless. I was human and deserving of love and compassion and my inner life, my inner monologue, my own little girl self, needed nurturing.

When my kids were in elementary school, in the spirit of classroom management, their teacher told them one day, "Words are like toothpaste in a tube. Once you say them or squeeze them out, there is no shoving them back in." The implication was of course that words can be damaging, and yes, that is true without a doubt. I knew it firsthand. And it's not just the words you say to others, it's what you say to yourself that can do harm. The problem with the toothpaste metaphor is that it implies that there is no opportunity to learn and change your inner monologue or your outer dialogue. The toothpaste is out and that is that. If you have chosen the wrong words, the damage is done and irreparable. But I disagree. Once we learn to practice self-love, we *can* change our words and rewrite our inner monologue, flipping the script, learning to reflect, to apologize, to connect, and to heal.

So many of us have to unlearn our internal vocabulary, untangle ourselves from our inner critics, and create a new dictionary. We can begin by saying one kind thing.

It's time to have a different conversation, to teach ourselves—maybe for the first time, or maybe all over again— that we are worthy, we are capable, we are enough.

CHAPTER 1

ALWAYS BEGINNING

It seems that from the moment I am awake each morning, my brain is busy. Like most people, I have a running to-do list of work, calls to be made, emails to be sent, deadlines coming up, bills to be paid. Then of course the kid's appointments, schedules, therapists, doctors, worries to be confronted, fires to be put out, conversations to be had, maybe squeezing in a little meditation or yoga. All of it running through my mind to be checked off as each task is accomplished. I like to have a predictable routine, and sometimes I feel like the more I have on my list, the more I get done. At the same time, I recognize that as much as I love to-do lists and planning, in reality, I never know what will be placed in front of me each day—the obstacles I will face, the lessons I will learn, or the tears I will cry. I have no idea if there will be something new and beautiful to see or feel. I have no idea and no way of controlling what might appear, interrupt, or shift what I pictured would be. Knowing this, and knowing myself, I intentionally pause and create a space in my busy brain before I launch into the day. I take a deep breath in and give myself a little pep talk: "Be easy on you. Be open. Be excited. The day is brand-new."

After years of practice and study and teaching mindfulness and yoga to kids, I often hear myself referred to as an "expert." Let me just *mindfully* pause right here and share what comes up for me around this title. I, like so many people, suffer from terrible impostor syndrome. Immediately, when anyone calls me an "expert" at *anything* my inner critic says, "Seriously? You? There must be some mistake! If only they knew. . . . Don't let them find out you are a total fraud." When I first hear this voice, I tend to believe it and I wonder what made me think I knew what I was talking about. Sometimes this will lead me down a rabbit hole of searching for yet another training that I can take or a book that I can read to justify that I *am* someone who knows enough . . . who is enough. Other times, I react to the voice in my head by retreating under the blanket of my anxiety, believing that I will never be good enough or know enough to be a true "expert." At these moments, I find myself unable to access any of my "tools," the ones I talk about so much and teach, and my lack of expertise is reinforced by my own behavior.

In my "expert" role, I visit schools to teach kids about mindfulness and self-care and how mindfulness can allow us to create a pause between ourselves and our emotions, making space for better choices, for responses rather than reactions, for being in the present moment. Kids especially are naturally open to these practices. They just get it, even as they giggle and fidget—they just soak it in. Together we embrace awkwardness, we meditate and breathe, and we explore the many ways to practice present moment awareness. I like to think that I am adding tools to their toolboxes and giving them options to help them navigate their lives.

Sometimes I get swept up in the beauty of sharing all of this with the kids, and when it's time for questions invariably one of them will bring *me* back to the present moment by asking, "Are YOU always mindful?" "Do YOU ever get angry or yell?" "Do YOU always stop and breathe?" Thank goodness for these questions. There I am standing in front of these little souls as an "expert," showing them all the things that will help them to love themselves, to handle big emotions, and to be the best they can be. And I completely forget to explain that we are *all* practicing and there is no such thing as ALWAYS, as PERFECT. No, I am not *always* calm and kind and fully present. I lose it. I yell. I get overwhelmed. I forget to breathe. Mindfulness isn't my default mode. It is something I have to reconnect with over and over again. My answer to them is always "No. No way. Absolutely not. That is why we call it a practice."

My own kids have a favorite story about me losing it over

something incredibly minute and unimportant in their eyes: my need for coffee. They find it hilarious to (lovingly) make fun of me for this, as they imitate me clutching my cup of coffee for dear life, saying things like "I don't care if the house is on fire, as long as I have my coffee!" Soon after all three of my kids were born, I started drinking coffee religiously. One of my parents would happily watch the kids while I took forty-five minutes for myself at our local coffee shop. These few minutes were heaven. As I've mentioned, I had mostly let my meditation and yoga practices go when I was a new mom. It was probably when I needed them the most, but I couldn't reach them. It felt like there was no time, no space. My coffee time became my meditation replacement. I recognize the irony here—getting jacked up on caffeine was probably the opposite of calming for my nervous system, but it was a few blissful moments in which to quiet my mind. And since my coffee runs were also an excuse to wear a spit-up-free shirt and an excuse to focus on something other than the consistency and frequency of poop, they became sacred.

I would sit at a specific corner table trying to think about nothing except the warm cup of coffee in my hands and my own quiet breath. This was how I told myself I was practicing. It's also how I kept myself connected to the world outside of myself and my messy, noisy, and often chaotic house filled with kids. This daily coffee time became my ritual. Initially it brought me some needed inner peace and calm. It gave me a break from mom duties, it gave me respite from a marriage that was starting to crumble, and it was forty-five minutes to just be. I only allowed myself forty-five minutes because any longer and a story would start in my brain about how I wasn't a present mother and was not allowed to put my own self-care ahead of my kids who needed me.

These forty-five minutes soon became something I *had* to have in order to function: a ritual that had been given so much importance. And eventually when the kids started school and I began writing children's books, it morphed into a time for me to get my work done. Embracing the caffeine buzz and clarity of mind, I would stay for longer and do more, and I would feel like someone other than a mom and wife. I could leave the stress of getting the kids ready for school and the arguments with my husband behind. I could set aside the never-ending needs of all of them and become someone else. Someone who was not failing, but who was making progress. I could tap into my creativity. I wrote many a manuscript sitting in this cozy coffee shop at the same table at the same time every day. It was the act around which my day was centered. The benefit of being a regular is that I developed a relationship with the baristas. They began to jokingly welcome me to my "office" when I would arrive and often made sure my favorite table was free. They were beautiful enablers.

By connecting this ritual to my ability to function, it made perfect sense that I would lose myself around my coffee habit. Getting the kids ready for school was always hectic, and as much as I would try to create an atmosphere of calm as I fed and clothed the three of them and got everyone out the door, it somehow never went smoothly. My ex would leave the house for work before anyone was awake and I would rise knowing there would most likely be a struggle to contend with—itchy clothes, worries about the day, general tiredness and crankiness. Jesse never liked going to school when they were little and at drop-off would sometimes break out of their classroom and run across the campus with the seventy-year-old security guard chasing after them. I knew they were safe and that an hour in they would be fine, but the possibility of a breakout was always there. Jacob had his rituals, which the therapist had told me I needed to interrupt, so I tried but was mostly unsuccessful. Poor Ben would just try to go with the flow and get to school on time. I (mostly) held it together because I love them, and also because I knew that soon enough, I would be sipping a latte with my laptop open and mind clear, peacefully creating.

On this particular morning, everyone was settled in the car, and we were on our way to school. After drop-off, I planned to go for coffee, as was my ritual. Our route to school took us right by the shop's entrance, which was always a beautiful sight, quietly beckoning me. But on this fateful day, when we drove by—BOOM—there was a big CLOSED sign hanging from the door. Not just closed until later, CLOSED ALL DAY!

Instantly, I felt sick to my stomach and burst into tears. With my foot still on the gas and gripping the wheel I started yelling about how my whole day was ruined. It was a full-on tantrum, a complete meltdown, the kind that if it happened in the grocery store with your kid you would leave your full cart behind and carry your kicking and screaming child out. I literally did not know how I would function that day without my ritual. The kids of course tried to comfort me, telling me it wasn't a big deal—I could make my coffee at home or go somewhere else. Coffee existed in the world outside of this coffee shop. But they couldn't reach me. I had turned into a crazy loon. I know I frightened them as I kept driving them to school, angrily ranting about how this *really* was a crisis and that they couldn't possibly understand.

Of course, they didn't understand. How could they? They didn't know the story going on in my head telling me I would fail on so many levels if I didn't get my latte at the right spot and how my "toolbox" was more like a safe whose combination I forgot. Where was my "expertise" then? Ultimately, I dropped the kids at school fighting back my tears and drove an extra forty-five minutes to a place in the next town over. I could have (God forbid) made my own coffee. But no—I needed to re-create something as close to my regular routine as possible. I remember on the way to an unfamiliar coffee place having anxiety about my order: Would they get it right? And then planning how I would react if they don't. Maybe I would just order it again, or maybe I would just have to breathe and drink the damn coffee.

So many times, in my life, when there has been an actual crisis, I have somehow mostly managed to be calm and collected. Instead of going into fight or flight, I find myself almost emotionless and clearheaded, able to consider what actions to take. I might cry and get upset after the fact, but in a true emergency, I am there with a level head. The time Jacob broke his arm while in Australia just as a global pandemic was beginning and he needed surgery with rods and pins, and I could only be on the phone with his doctors and not there in person . . . I was cool as a cucumber. When Jesse split their face open on a piece of ice and I had to drive them to the hospital alone with blood gushing from their upper lip . . . I was calm and collected. When Ben broke his ankle and also needed surgery (oy vey, so many broken bones) . . . I was focused and ready. Even when I found out my father was dying of pancreatic cancer . . . somehow, despite the sadness and fear, I was able to think and proceed clearly and intentionally and stepped in to care for him. There wasn't time to create a scenario or to attach my self-worth to these things. There were no rituals and compulsions established. But a closed coffee shop? I lost it in an embarrassing and crazy way.

The kids and I laugh about it now, and I have been able to share with them what was really happening in my brain back then. They are old enough to get it, and they still think I was hilariously insane. In that moment, however, I was totally lost, incapable of explaining anything. Swept up in the chaos of my mind, I was unable to find the words. Today I recognize that my coffee time had become inextricably linked to my ability to function as a mother with three kids at home and a husband who always seemed critical and controlling. Coffee time was my way to create some space for myself, a quick refueling. Then it became linked to my ability to write. The need to control things, combined with the remnants of my childhood struggle with OCD, had created a connection between the details of my coffee time and my ability to write. Following through on these compulsions ensured I would get some writing done. Again, the story in my brain.

In that moment, what I also couldn't see or put into words was how far down the road of my inevitable terrible future my mind went. No coffee from the right spot with the right foam at the right time would lead to instant writer's block, no more books, no more career, no more income, which would then disappoint my agent, my editor, my mother, my children, and, of course, myself, which would lead to everyone finding out that I am in fact an imposter. This is literally what my brain told me. I could only fuel my ideas with *this* routine, *this* coffee. My kids like to end this story by pointing out that I wasn't very mindful that day. No, I was not.

Now, when the kids I teach ask me if I am always mindful or if I ever get upset, I think of this story. And there are other stories too. There is nothing like parenting to make you feel like a total "non-expert." I was talking to a friend of mine who is a new father and he said, "This parenting thing, does anyone really know how to do it? I think it's actually all improv." I laughed and had never thought about it that way, but it is so true. I feel like I am always onstage and saying to the audience (aka children and the universe) "Give me a location, a character, a scenario!" And then I am to act out a scene that somehow makes sense.

NYC hospital. Twin boys. Induced birth. GO!

New home. Another baby. Unstable marriage. GO!

Rental house. Middle school boy with OCD. GO!

Global pandemic. Teenage child. Transgender coming out. GO!

Boarding school in Florida. Football accident. Major surgery. GO!

Small things and big things thrown at you all day long from one minute to the next. Before having kids, I had the audacity to think that it was possible to become an expert at parenting. I thought I knew what NOT to do, and that would lead me to know what TO do. I knew not to dismiss my kids. I knew not to ignore them or make them feel like their emotions and opinions weren't valid. I knew to be present and patient. But even knowing all of this wasn't enough to prepare me for *every* situation, or allow me to understand *every* cry or need, or feel like I had it all under control. With parenting, I quickly discovered that I was an amateur, a beginner at every stage. How had I gotten this gig without being more prepared for it? Every day it was something different. Every day was a new emotion, situation, or experience. Only by leaning into the newness of every moment, by accepting that I was a constant beginner, could I begin to let go of the idea that I *should* know, in order to make way for trying without judgment. Sometimes I would get it right and sometimes I wouldn't, but either way, I could stay open to learning.

Immediately after my coffee meltdown, I was frustrated with myself and embarrassed. With so many "real" things in the world to get upset about, was I really losing it over coffee? I had scared my kids. I had failed to access my "tools"—mindfulness, breathing, talking to myself with kindness and compassion. Instead, I had turned into a raving loon who couldn't stop the swirling tornado of thoughts in her head. What was I modeling for my kids? After the way I'd behaved, how could I stand in front of other kids and talk about mindfulness, self-care, and self-compassion? What kind of "expert" was I?

There is a concept in Zen Buddhism called beginner's mind, and although I have not formally studied Buddhism, it is a concept I have grown familiar with through my yoga and meditation training. Beginner's mind is the practice of looking at life through the eyes of a beginner, where each moment or experience seems new or has a quality of newness. When you practice this kind of thinking, the mundane can become interesting and even exciting. The unknown or unplanned can become less scary and an opportunity to learn. You can tap into a sense of wonder and curiosity rather than seeing your mistakes as failures. Perhaps, if I had remembered to access my beginner's mind that day when the coffee shop was closed, instead of instantly berating myself and telling myself that I was a fraud for reacting the way I did, instead of shutting down and closing myself off, I would have approached the experience with curiosity and self-compassion, understanding all that I had attached to the situation that had nothing at all to do with coffee. Perhaps I would have been able to even see the humor in it. Today, with a beginner's mind, I can think back to that morning, consider my reaction, and let it go—knowing that I will be given the opportunity to try again. Thinking like a beginner on that day might not have prevented the meltdown, but it would have allowed me an opportunity to learn from the experience and to give myself some grace.

When it comes to managing our emotions, can we ever really become experts? Do we even want to be? We demand perfection from ourselves, and we model this for our children, all the while knowing that it is not attainable. We compare ourselves to others. We forget to embrace the joy in *not* knowing. We forget about the excitement of beginning. The way the world is for a child. If we knew that there was nothing left to learn, that we were never going to make another mistake, or face another setback, would we be OK with that? Would we really want to live that way?

Maybe the most important thing I can share with my own kids and the kids I teach—my nonexpert/expert's advice—is to hold onto your beginner's mind. Approach each moment as if it is brand-new and stay open to that newness. You have the tools within you to breathe, to be present, to make choices, and to be kind to yourself. You can practice using these tools, knowing that you will inevitably mess it up and will have to start again, try again. Instead of seeking perfection, looking for an outcome, going through the motions because you think you've been here and done this before, embrace curiosity and wonder. See what you can discover and what there is to learn, feel, and experience in each moment when you are a beginner. Maybe this is the most important advice I can give to myself: Tap into my beginner's mind. Wake each morning realizing that I may have lists and goals and coffee cravings but really, I don't know what lies ahead. And in the unknown I can take a breath, inhaling the excitement of a day full of possibility.

In this moment,
everything is new, and
I am full of wonder.

CHAPTER 2

A HAND
TO HOLD

A few years back I went to a spin class and when I arrived at the studio, everyone was standing in the hall grumbling and complaining. The teacher was late, but so was I (as usual). I was just relieved that I hadn't missed anything. Eventually, the instructor flew in the door and declared, "I am so sorry I am late! My kid was having a meltdown and I couldn't stop it! I finally just stuck the iPad in his face so I could get out the door. I know, I know, I am the worst mother ever, right?" This last part she said with nervous laughter, and all the other moms in the room knew exactly what she was feeling: The expectation she had put on herself about being able to calm the tantrums without using electronics or yelling or getting frustrated because that is what a "good" mother would be able to do. My instinct was to go give her a hug and say, "It's OK. I've been there. You are doing great!" But like everyone else in the class, I avoided eye contact, got on my bike, and started pedaling.

After class, I couldn't stop thinking about that moment, wishing I had said something or even just smiled and nodded like "I hear you, sister!" So many times, on this motherhood journey, I have been in that place, berating myself for a choice I made or some perceived failure. I regretted my silence.

When my babies were in my belly and they were more of a concept than a reality, I felt like I was destined to be a great mom. I did all the things one is told to do for their kids when they are *in utero*. I tried to eat well. I read to them and sang and told them how amazing they were. I set up their nursery with the proper mobiles and toys to stimulate them and make sure they were hitting all the milestones: everything the books said to do. And I had plans about how we would be together as a family. Minimal screen time, if any; only organic foods; and of course breastfeeding for as long as possible. I had the chance to give them what I hadn't gotten, and I would always put them first. I would be such a good mom that it would drown out my feelings of inadequacy, of not being a good enough daughter, and of not being a good enough person. I had been working on myself and these feelings for so many years and now I could put it all into action with my own children.

But as soon as my kids entered the world with their tears and needs, there were so many ways in which I seemed to be straying from the plan. I had made a list based on my pre-birth plan: no screen time, breastfeeding for at least the first year, only healthy foods after that, a regular sleep schedule, and more. In reality: They never slept (they still don't sleep) and neither did I. I had trouble breastfeeding and had to switch to bottles before six months. I thanked God for screens, I lost socks in the street, I forgot diapers when we left the house, and pass the chicken nuggets, please. I quickly realized that just keeping everyone alive, including myself, was the best I could do. I found myself angry at the authors of all the parenting books I had read. Why had nobody prepared me for this? I wasn't the type to join a moms' group, and I wondered, were other moms having these same experiences and sharing them with each other? Would I have even wanted a fellow mom to warn me that once I had my babies I'd feel inadequate? I had loved being pregnant, so I might not have listened. Was this why nobody had told me? In my head, it was all my fault. I was flawed.

When the twins were just little ones, before my third was born, I took the two of them to the grocery store for one of our first public outings. In honor of the occasion, I had somehow managed to shower and dress myself in something other than sweats or the paneled pregnancy jeans that still felt good against my belly. I dressed the boys in cute little outfits and made sure I was well equipped with wipes, bottles, pacifiers, toys—all the gear. I got them in their car seats and we headed to the store. I was so happy to get out of the house and to feel like I was accomplishing things with babies in tow.

When we got to the grocery store, I put them in their giant double stroller, grabbed my canvas shopping bag and the diaper bag, and headed inside, trying so hard to have it all together. The instant I walked through the doors, Jacob started crying. He had slumped down in his seat the way he always did when in the stroller and was just sobbing his little eyes out. But I was determined to complete this task. I gave him his pacifier and tried distracting him with my out-of-tune singing and dangling toys in front of him. I told myself this was normal baby behavior, that I should not be embarrassed, and that I was going to get these groceries. As I moved quickly through the aisles with a now screaming child, most people thankfully ignored me, and I tried to hide my anxiety and avoid eye contact with anyone.

As I headed down the final aisle, an elderly woman approached us. In my mind, I see her as a crazy-eyed witchy lady with long gray hair who had flown in on a broomstick and dropped down in front of me. She started shouting, literally shouting, much louder than Jacob's screaming. "What is wrong with you? Look at your child! He is obviously in pain! Look at the way you are letting him sit in his stroller. No wonder he is crying! You should be ashamed! You are a terrible mother!"

When I was pregnant, I received a lot of unsolicited advice, none of it helpful and none that prepared me for an encounter like this one. I had many strangers place their hands on my belly without asking, and most of what they said was harmless—questions about how far along I was, some oohing and aahing, tips they thought I might appreciate. Even when it felt like a violation of my personal space, it was never anything critical. Having someone scream at me was new, however.

I recall muttering an apology to the woman, and saying "Yes, yes, of course you are right." I bent down in front of the stroller, trying desperately to straighten my child so he wouldn't be "in pain." That is when the inner reprimands began:

How could you not have tried harder? Maybe he is in pain!

What is wrong with you?

What kind of mother are you?

Every time I sat Jacob up, he would slump down again. I had conveniently forgotten the number of times he had ridden around peacefully in this same stroller in this same position. No, I was obviously torturing him. It was me, my fault.

In this moment, all my determination to be better and do better, all the ways in which I felt competent and confident as a mom, went out the window. I instantly took on the words of the world, the words of this screaming stranger. I desperately wanted to be the mother who would prove that she could do it all and do it right. But instead, I went right back to being the little girl who was "worthless." I stood there feeling like a reprimanded child. I abandoned my groceries and hurried the twins in their double stroller out of the store, with the words "terrible mother" replaying on a loop in my brain.

Back home, Jacob's hysterical crying finally stopped and mine began. I had to talk to someone, and so I picked up the phone and called my mother. Part of me was afraid to tell her what had happened. I didn't want her to see me as failing, once again the daughter who had disappointed her. Would she also think I was a terrible mother? But I needed her, so I took the risk. I told her the story of what had happened, humiliated that I had not been able to handle a simple trip to the grocery store with the twins. I wondered what her reaction would be. I'd heard my mother's stories about *her* own mother. They'd never had an emotional connection and they didn't really talk about things when my mom was growing up. They certainly never spoke about their worries or much of anything below the surface. I knew that if my mother had felt unsure of herself as a new mother or even as my brother and I got older, my grandmother would not have been the person she'd call.

When I was a child, my mother had limited patience for strong emotions of any kind from her kids. My father was more willing to take on the tears and the tantrums, maybe because he himself was a highly emotional, and often an explosive, person. My mother would try to get things to end as soon as possible with distraction rather than validation, and when that didn't work, she retreated to her bedroom. Perhaps it was easier on her psyche to create distance. Engaging with us emotionally wasn't something she was prepared to take, maybe because she'd had no model for handling emotions of any kind, and especially those of children. She was, however, the MOST wonderful grandmother. There was a love there that seemed to fill her soul and she had patience for almost anything that her grandchildren threw her way. In this moment, however, when I was the one who needed her, I wasn't entirely sure how she would react. Would my emotion overwhelm her? Would she judge me for what had gone down in the grocery store? Or would she relate? Would she show me compassion?

She listened to me tearfully share my grocery store experience, and then she asked, "Did it ever occur to you that Jacob likes that position, and maybe he was crying for another reason? Or no reason at all? You are not a terrible mother; you are just A MOTHER." She also added that I should have told the lady to F— off, which looking back I wish I had done. In that moment, *she* was a GREAT mother and I started to think of how hard it all must have been for her too, and how maybe no one had been there to show *her* compassion or tenderness.

She was right, I *am* just a mother. Not "just "in the sense that

I am ONLY a mother and nothing else, or that being a mother is something small and insignificant like "It's *just* a flesh wound." She meant it more as in, I am BEING a mother, and the fears and mistakes and uncertainties are what mothering is about. The ache in your heart and the inability to control and fix and predict—that's the job. It's not about perfection or doing it all right. I thanked her and hung up the phone feeling supported and grateful. She gave me just what I needed.

Once I was a little older and wiser, and my kids were old enough to dole out sarcasm, whenever one of us noticed that I'd made a parenting "mistake" or misstep, we would say, "Oh well, that was an A+ for parenting!" It became a running family joke. The time I showed them Michael Jackson's "Thriller" video when they were little and it scared the daylights out of them: A+. The time I forgot to feed them lunch: A+. It became a way for all of us to laugh together, to acknowledge that this thing called life isn't easy, and to embrace imperfection.

It was great to feel at times like we were all in this together, but as my kids edged closer to middle school, I knew the day would come when one of them would tell me they hated me. I was waiting for it. I remember saying it to my own parents as a preteen and really feeling it in the moment. I had also seen it happen with friends and their kids, so I was ready. I almost felt like it was a rite of passage. It was Jesse who said it first. Jesse, old and wise for their years. I don't remember what I did to set them off, but I do remember they said, very loudly and publicly: "I hate you!!!" And then, for emphasis, followed up with "And not only do I hate you. . . . EVERYONE hates you!" Surprisingly, this did not make me feel like a terrible mother. It made me laugh and appreciate my child even more for the extra effort. Though of course, in the moment, I had to keep a straight face and pretend I was horribly offended.

As my kids grew, it wasn't the yelling or the telling me they hated me that could make me feel like a bad parent. It wasn't the fact that after fourth grade I was no longer capable of helping them with their math homework that I didn't understand. It wasn't the swearing (which they have learned from me) or the door slamming. It wasn't the fact that I am an awful cook and refuse to prepare a big meal for holidays like Thanksgiving (which no one in our family likes anyway). It's the things I can't fix that make me feel like a bad mom. The things I can't prevent. The problems I can't solve. It's Jacob's struggle with OCD. It's the fallout from my divorce and that I felt their father isn't present. It's Jesse's feelings of loneliness in school or the pandemic keeping friends away from friends and family away from family.

I feel like I am a bad mom when, in the middle of a reprimand, I realize that I am projecting my own fears onto a situation. I hear myself telling my child they can't eat something, not because it's bad for them but because I remember eating my feelings as a young person, putting on weight, and heading into a spiral of self-loathing. I catch myself hovering and harping on a point instead of just saying "No" or "Don't." I find myself stuck in a loop of overexplaining, not giving my kids credit for what they already know, as in "I don't want you eating dinner at midnight, not because I think it will hurt you per se, but because it's not good for your digestion and blah blah blah . . ." I feel like a bad mom when I see my kids experiencing sadness or pain, but I know that I can't make it all better. I'm right back in that moment where no matter how much I try to straighten them in the stroller, I can't change anything, I can't stop the crying.

Now that my children are teenagers, they are pulling away from me and there is nothing I can do to stop it. I know this is meant to be. People tell me that if your kids are pulling away, it means that you've done your job. I have given them the confidence to separate from me and cultivate their own identity, blah, blah, blah. Intellectually I know that is true but sometimes in the dark places of my mind I still feel like it must be because deep down I am a terrible mother and I have made them feel like they must leave me. And that is a feeling I find myself fighting.

Like my spin instructor, I find myself confessing. This is a common practice among moms—"confessing," as if we need to admit to the world that we are inadequate moms, so that we can then feel unburdened by our perceived mistakes. Responding to a confessing mom is tricky business. We want commiseration without condescension. We don't want pity or judgment, just support and maybe a reminder that this too shall pass. All of this mixed in with a bit of humor. We just want to be seen. However, in my experience, people tend to respond in a way that offers advice, and that can sound a bit judgey. This is why, over the years, I have learned to be careful about who I "confess" to. I think carefully about who I might talk to for support. Either that, or I blurt things out in passing to people who I know won't respond, kind of like my spin teacher did. Sometimes confessing to a roomful of strangers who won't respond is easier than talking to people we know. There is less of a chance you will be judged or pitied or that they will even remember, and you can unburden yourself a bit more freely.

Soon after that spin incident, I was in yoga class, and I encountered another confessing mom. She and I were friendly, though not close friends. We spoke of our kids and our exes but mostly kept it light. We did not spend time together outside of class, not for any particular reason but just because our lives went in different directions. She was my yoga buddy. Typically, in class, she was a person filled with humor and sarcasm and I loved our pre-class chats and laughs but this day she was visibly not herself. As we unrolled our mats she began confessing. She was having trouble with her teenage son. She told me the details of his depression and that he was sliding into addiction and how she felt like a terrible mother. She had not been able to fix things and she felt like his suffering was all her fault.

I knew the last thing she needed was pity or advice, which would only reinforce her inner voice telling her she was failing. I knew exactly what she was going through. These are the situations where words of judgment and self-criticism enter us. When we feel powerless to fix or prevent or anticipate. Previously, with the spin instructor, I had imagined telling her I get it and it was all OK, but I chose to stay quiet with the rest of the class. It was *not* her fault. She was doing the best she could. She was a great mom. That was the truth. But I didn't say anything. I wish I had. This time, with my yoga friend, I was ready to say these things out loud. However, as soon as my friend told me her story, class began and so did our silent practice. I hadn't gotten a chance to say anything. Maybe that was why she'd confessed all of this to me so close to the start of class. Maybe she was not looking for a response, knowing there would not be time for one. Still, I wanted her to know that she wasn't alone in these thoughts. I wanted to show her the understanding and compassion I hadn't had the guts to show the spin teacher, and that I certainly hadn't shown myself.

I think of a yoga class as a place to go for healing. Yoga is where I began my own healing journey, and it got me through many of the most difficult times in my life. Often, people tear up during class when something is released in their bodies. It can be an emotional experience. But there are rules in most adult classes. Unlike kids' yoga classes that are noisy and full of talking and laughter and sometimes chaos, yoga for grown-ups is a place where the inner work is done in silence. Our mats are our own little islands and though we feed off the energy of others practicing around us, we maintain our distance and try to find connection to ourselves.

The only sounds that followed were breathing, the voice of the teacher and the music. But as I practiced that morning, my brain was noisy. I felt the depth of my friend's words and knew them all too well. I thought about the spin instructor and my silence in that moment and the silence of all the moms in the class. I thought about the confessions and the feelings of failure we all keep quiet. I knew that at the end of class there wouldn't be any lingering. As we always did, we would all be quickly rolling up our mats and heading out into our lives. But I didn't want my friend to leave without knowing she wasn't alone.

As we came to the final minutes of class and lay down on our backs in savasana, I decided to break the rules. We were meant to lie there in reflection, silently focusing on the weight of our bodies and the depth of our breathing. Instead, I reached my hand across the space between us and I grabbed my friend's hand, not knowing if she would take it or gently nudge it away. She held tight. I held tight. Soon our breathing was in sync. No pity. No judgment. No labels. Just us. We held on for the next few minutes until class was over. Then in silence we rolled up our mats and went back out into the real world of our busy lives.

What I hope she knew in that moment was that I understood. That I also struggled with showing myself tenderness, forgiving the mistakes, and countering the words of failure that sometimes filled my brain. I was holding her hand, but she was also holding mine. We held each other in that moment, we saw each other in that moment. The smallest gesture became a lifeline, a safety net, an exhale. The space we created for each other, holding hands, was filled only with connection and compassion. We were not good mothers or terrible mothers. We were *just* two mothers, being.

I have compassion for myself;
just *being* is enough.

CHAPTER 3

GIVING THANKS

Another Thanksgiving has passed. Since my father's death more than five years ago, the kids and I haven't celebrated. We haven't even tried. There are many reasons I can come up with to justify why we don't "do" Thanksgiving. With my father gone, and Ben staying at boarding school over the breaks for football practices, and my mother often choosing to spend the holiday with old friends, there are too many missing people. In addition, none of us like turkey or mashed potatoes or any of the traditional holiday foods, and with my own eating issues, a holiday that is spent *over*eating just doesn't appeal to me.

When I was growing up, we always celebrated Thanksgiving. Our tradition was to bring our dishes to the home of my parents' best friends every year. My father would make his "famous" mashed potatoes and my mother would make squash soup and pumpkin pie. Food wasn't the issue for me back then. Until I turned fifteen or so, I was relatively free from the body dysmorphia and disordered eating that would ultimately shape my unhealthy relationship with food. To me, the torture was that this holiday was never relaxed, never easy or joyful. My brother and I were required to dress up, and I remember the feeling of itchy stockings and snug-fitting dresses and my hair pulled back in a too-tight bow. We sat around quietly eating while the adults drank heavily, and we kids tried to hang in there until we were dismissed to another room to watch TV. That was the only good part. That and the sandwiches my dad made for himself when we got home with leftover turkey, potato chips, and mayo on white bread. We would sit on the couch together in our pj's laughing, asking our dad, "How can you eat even more?"

When I was in middle school my father and I started another tradition of going for a run along the West Side Highway before we headed to Thanksgiving dinner. We were always at our best when we were exercising together. I like to think that somewhere deep down neither of us enjoyed the stiff and uptight "celebration" that lay ahead, and the running and endorphins helped us both cope.

My parents' friends' apartment was too neat and too sterile. There was too much alcohol and there were no other kids. And there was always the presence of the father of one of my parents' friends, a lecherous older man who grew more handsy and inappropriate with every year. My sophomore year in high school when my brother was away at college and had made the smart choice not to come home for the holiday, I was alone in my misery and also found myself alone with this awful old man. With alcohol on his breath, he got too close. I literally had to push him off of me as he groped me in the kitchen. That was it! I had had enough. I left without a word and went to my best friend's apartment, where we snuck out and smoked weed in her elevator. I swore I'd never go back to those Thanksgiving dinners with my parents, and I never did. They never questioned why I left that night or why I wouldn't go back. Maybe they figured I was old enough to choose or maybe it just wasn't worth the argument. Either way, I was done with Thanksgiving.

When the kids were babies, we decided to try again, hoping to start a family tradition that was more relaxed and casual. My parents hosted all of us at their house, so that we could easily leave when the kids melted down, and their father and I could avoid the burden of cleaning up. It was better. There was some laughter and some fun. We didn't need to dress up and wore whatever was comfy and could handle the spills and spit-ups that were inevitable. But still, it was challenging. At that point, the idea of encountering so much food was overwhelming for me, and really, I was so focused on the kids that it didn't ever end up feeling like a celebration, just an obligation and a chore. Over the next few years, we tried to keep it going, even hosting at our house once, but by the time the kids were toddlers, we gave up. The most we could muster was to stop by my parents' house for a couple of hours without sitting and suffering through a meal.

Today, my kids have accepted the fact that I am not interested in Thanksgiving traditions, other than the Thanksgiving exercise tradition started with my dad, which means taking an extra-long "gratitude" yoga class or a ninety-minute spin class aptly named the "turkey burn" to clear my mind for the rest of the day. The kids all seem to be more than fine with forfeiting this holiday. I have heard them explain to others the reasons why we don't celebrate, parroting my reasons: not everyone is home, it's too sad without grandpa, and none of us like turkey.

While all of these things are true, there is also another reason why we don't celebrate this holiday or any other holiday that asks all of us to sit down together at a table. It's the same reason we don't take family vacations or family photos or family car rides.

When Jacob was four years old, he was diagnosed with OCD. It was something I suffered from as a child as well but had never been diagnosed and I didn't really know what it was until it appeared in my own child. Although I probably started showing signs when I was very little, I don't remember noticing that there was something different about me until I was eight. I went to the movies with my mom, and it turned out that I had a terrible stomach virus, which resulted in me puking all over the theater. It was traumatizing to say the least. From that moment on I was terrified to be in crowds or at the movies and created rituals to help with my anxiety.

No one really understood what was happening and it was just annoying for the people around me. When I was invited to birthday parties that involved going to the movies (which were popular when I was a kid), I would find an excuse to sit in the lobby until it was over.

Somehow in my teens I seemed to get a better handle on it. Perhaps because in order to have friends and any kind of social life, I had to expose myself to the things that made me anxious. Or maybe I was better able to hide my anxiety. Eventually with therapy and a better understanding of what was happening and of myself, it morphed into what it is today, ever present but not as strong. When the ruminations start and the thoughts come into my head, even if I can't get rid of them completely, I am able to recognize what is happening and counter these thoughts or sit with them, even when they are loud. However, it isn't this way for my son.

I know he must have inherited his OCD from me but then added his own special genetic sauce. In the beginning, it was just some little quirks. What seemed to me like regular kid stuff. As a toddler, he didn't like scratchy clothes and we filled his drawers with seamless socks and tagless everything. He had little behaviors, like pushing up his sleeves repeatedly or counting toilet paper squares, that I learned to interrupt before they became rituals. It felt manageable and I thought I was on top of it. But when Jacob was six, the rituals and compulsions kicked into full gear. As he experienced it, his brain started telling him stories of fear and danger, which led to him performing complicated routines that he believed would determine the outcome of his day. He would wake up in the morning and have to jump from his top bunk and land in a very particular way on the trundle bed below. If this didn't go well, he would have to start over. If it did go well then it was on to the next action of kicking off his pajama bottoms and catching them in his right hand with one eye closed. If this didn't go well it was back to the bunk bed. If it did go well then it was off with the shirt, spin in a couple of circles, and toss the pj's into a mini basketball hoop we had set up in the kitchen and THEN off to school. If this didn't go just right his brain told him something bad would happen and he would need to start again back at the jumping off the bunk bed.

This was the story his brain was telling him. At first, I felt incredibly guilty that he had inherited this struggle from me. By the time we got to school each morning, he and I would both be in tears. Ben and Jesse learned to live with it as part of our morning routine—this was Jacob. Finally, his teacher let me off the hook by telling me that I should just send him to school in his pj's and pack some other clothes, in case he wanted to change during the day. But no need to force it, this was not a battle worth fighting. So, although I was likely enabling him, he spent a year in pajamas all day every day and another in pajama bottoms and a regular shirt. This was progress and with the help of a therapist he was doing better, ultimately wearing almost anything, with the exception of socks with seams.

Then it all took an even more complicated and terrible turn. In fifth grade his OCD brain latched onto Jesse. Suddenly he would scream with sheer terror whenever Jesse was near, hiding behind his brother or running to his room. Jesse was a lefty, so Jacob stopped using the left side of his upper body. Whenever we were all together, he could never be right next to Jesse. It was chaos. And it was nearly impossible to explain to his school, to friends, or even to my parents. None of it made sense. Everyone handed over their pity, but there were no answers.

Not only was Jacob suffering, but Jesse was silently falling apart, wondering what they had done wrong. Jesse and Jacob had once been so close, and suddenly Jacob couldn't be near them or say their name. In his brain, Jesse had scary magical powers that could harm him. Jesse's self-esteem tanked, the rift between them was growing, and I couldn't do anything to stop it. Ben became the buffer, the one who would be in the middle physically, and the one who Jacob turned to for support. If Ben was present, Jacob felt safe. Ben responded by always being positive and trying to balance his relationship with both of them, while focusing on his own life and goals. On the outside he was easier, but there was a lot happening on the inside and he needed support too.

I knew when I had kids that they—like me, like all of us—would at some point hear things in their minds that didn't reflect who they were, that weren't true, that would cause them to get in their own way. That is being human. I figured that if I could give them the right tools and vocabulary, if I modeled how I do this for myself, if I spoke to them in the right way, they would be able to recognize a "real" thought and a false one. That they could learn to determine what was helpful and what would hold them back. It had taken me a long time to get to a place where I could do this for myself. I thought that if I could teach them about this early, they wouldn't have damage to undo like I had. But for Jacob, the OCD was too strong. There were some thoughts that he could counter and quiet, but the thoughts he was having about Jesse were deafening.

On the outside, in front of my kids, I wasn't going to give up or give in to this. But inside, my mind filled with words, thoughts, judgments. *Why is this happening? You are a failure. You caused this. You are being punished because you are worthless. Being there for all three of your kids is not a task that you are capable of handling.* There were already so many things about parenting that challenged the way I spoke to myself, but this felt crazy and impossible.

Then I became fixated on fixing. Next came meds, exposure therapy, pulling Jacob from school to go to clinics with doctors who claimed to know what they were doing and only caused more damage. And when things weren't working, when nothing was changing, I focused on hating. Blaming the OCD. Hating it. It ruined my plans. It got in the way of what I set out to do with my family. It F-ed up my chance to prove to myself that I could create a family with no damage, children with no trauma, because I was smarter, I had done the work and could do better. I wallowed in feeling helpless and hopeless.

One incredibly difficult day, I found Jacob in his room crying. It wasn't unusual for him to show his emotions, but the questions he asked that day were new. *Why am I like this? What is wrong with me? I really love them (unable to say Jesse's name but getting their pronouns right), but I can't show them. Sometimes I hate myself. Am I a bad person?*

Oh, God. This is exactly what I never wanted for any of my kids to feel about themselves. There was an almost unbearable ache. I held him close for a long time and some part of me was hoping I could absorb all his pain and take it away. OCD is a monster. It's not always about organizing and handwashing, as it's glibly portrayed, and even those acts go deeper than what is on the surface. It doesn't look the same for everyone. It's not the thing of jokes. It makes no sense. Even if you know when it started or what triggered it you can't "cure" it by talking it out. And sometimes all the things that are supposed to help don't. Even now—when my son is mature enough to intellectually understand that his thoughts are irrational and that his beliefs are magical and superstitious, even when he's filled with remorse and the desire to stop his rituals and compulsions and to be able to be with Jesse—he can't stop the feelings. At least not yet.

I have three unique humans under my roof, in my care, who need to know they are each loved and amazing. They need to know that everyone has their sh*t and that it doesn't define them at their core. They need to know that they don't need fixing as they aren't broken. Life is about working on ourselves with compassion and forgiveness. When we focus on "fixing" or get caught up in anger and blame, beauty and wonder and gratitude get lost. Jacob is my reminder that my job as a mother and as a person is to be present and to accept what is. Like everyone else on this planet, Jacob will keep working and trying and loving the best he can, remembering that we need darkness and struggle to experience love and the light.

The OCD doesn't follow us everywhere. It doesn't always dominate. Each one of my kids laughs and loves. They have amazing friends and relationships. They are kind and creative. They are socially conscious and mindful. They engage with life fully. And when the OCD is present in our family, we are learning to work around it and with it without blame or shame. *We* have learned to celebrate the small wins, the baby steps, as much as we do the big ones.

Maybe one day, Jacob and Jesse will be able to repair their relationship. Maybe one day they will go to each other's weddings or sit at each other's dinner tables or lean on each other when they are struggling. Maybe one day they will be able to talk about it all and really express the love and the sadness that exists and has been there all along. Maybe one day they will help someone else who is feeling the same pain. There is always a chance for healing. But I don't put my faith in the future, not because I don't want these things to be so, but because we are here in this moment. This is what we have, now, and this is how we face it, moment by moment, step by step. We keep going. We keep being. We keep growing. OCD doesn't define us.

Our "family time" does not look like other families. But instead of forcing ourselves into the "should" box and keeping up appearances at everyone's expense, we choose something else. Jacob's OCD aside, I would still have done family holidays differently, as those past Thanksgiving experiences were never ones I wanted to replicate. If there were no OCD, yes, I would love for all of us to have more family time together. But this is what we have, and we are making the most of it, without having to explain ourselves. For now, we don't have family dinners. We don't go on family road trips. We don't take family photos and we don't celebrate Thanksgiving. We *do* have one-on-one dinners. We *do* take trips but separately. We *do* take plenty of pictures. We do what we can. No less meaningful. No less important. No less joyful. And still a celebration of our family.

I don't spend my time wishing that these things were different or for my family or my kids to be different. I don't tell myself that I have failed my children or that I have failed myself. This is our challenge. We are works in progress, and this is our family, whatever it looks like today. We have so much. Screw Thanksgiving!

I find gratitude in
choosing to celebrate
what works for me.

CHAPTER 4

you ARE HERE

am not a mall person. I prefer a city block lined with shops, the destination of a single store, or a charming outdoor stand selling artisan goods. (Who doesn't?) But sometimes I am in a place where mall shopping is the only option. I don't love malls because they are sensory overload. I also have trouble navigating such a big overwhelming space, and I find myself constantly stopping to orient myself at those giant mall maps, which only leaves me more confused about where the shops are exactly. Thank God for the marker on the map that says "YOU ARE HERE." Each time I read that I breathe a serious sigh of relief and I no longer feel lost. I know where *I* am. I am HERE. I am in this place, in this spot, in this moment even if I never find the damn shoe store.

I don't teach yoga to adults. I have done all the trainings, from trauma to prenatal. I have learned all about the history of yoga, I've studied the chants and the Sanskrit, and I have lovingly soaked it all up. I have subbed as an adult yoga teacher here and there. But something has always stopped me from becoming a full-time yoga teacher for grown-ups. I would rather practice with adults and teach to kids. They are less intimidating, and I love the idea that I can give them tools early on, before they start to believe that the troubling thoughts in their heads define who they are. There is also the fact that I am still working on the arm balances and headstands and all the things that I felt I needed to be able to do well or at all to teach adults. Maybe this is an example of self-judgment stopping me, and it's something I need to work on alongside my headstand. However, with kids, mistakes are part of the process and embracing this feels more natural to me than being able to do a perfect arm balance.

On a recent morning I took a yoga class with a teacher friend and while I was in savasana she gave me some words, a mantra to say to myself. The night before I'd had a heated phone conversation with Ben, who is away at boarding school, and I was holding onto some mistakes in the way I'd handled it. My mind had been racing and I had taken over the conversation. Ben kept saying "chill" and "you need to relax," words that only made things worse in a situation that was triggering my emotions. I, of course, did need to do both of these things, but my brain was not allowing it. Ben has been going to boarding school for the past four years, and even though you would think I'd be used to the separation at this point, I still miss him as though he just left. The physical distance creates a perceived emotional distance on my end, and sometimes I forget that he is a teenager who naturally doesn't want to share his every inner thought with his mother. If he were at home, I would most likely be annoyed by his withdrawal but also take it in stride. But with him away, sometimes I feel so desperate to connect that I push too hard and try to make him see how necessary I am. This is what happened on the phone. By the end of the call, I was yelling and he was yelling and instead of being supportive or interested or even allowing space for him to share, I was lost in a story of my own making.

The next morning, I was berating myself. Why can't I just relax? Why do I need to control everything, knowing I can't control anything? Have I made it so that Ben will never share anything with me again? As soon as my yoga class began and my friend asked me how I was, the tears came, and I shared the story that was playing on a loop in my brain. "The best way to get out of your head is to get into your body," she said, and so, teary-eyed, we began practice. As I moved and listened to my breath, I started to feel things fall away. At the end of our physical practice, when I was lying in relaxation, she said: "Repeat after me . . . I am doing so much better than my mind is telling me." Suddenly, I was able to return to myself. By the time it was over, I was different, calmer, with a little more perspective, and forgiveness and compassion to offer my busy, over-thinking mind. This is why I love yoga so much.

I wrote a children's book that is specifically yoga focused, that is a reworking of the fairy tale "The Three Little Pigs." The premise of the book is that the wolf loses his ability to huff and puff but still feels angry and doesn't know how to channel his anger. He happens upon three little yogi piggies who help him feel better through yoga and mindfulness. Although it has gotten many great reviews and seems to be resonating with kids, teachers, and parents it also got one terrible, mean-spirited, hurtful review, which is of course the one that has stuck with me. The anonymous reviewer was not just upset, he seemed to be downright huff and puff angry. One of the many awful things he said in his review was (to paraphrase) that the tone of my book was elitist, and that I was suggesting that being enlightened through yoga could solve all of one's problems and it went on from there.

In my defense, it was specifically a YOGA book with YOGA in the title so to expect anything else, including additional anger management tips or a disclaimer of some kind at the front of the book, was a bit ridiculous. After I got over the blow to my ego, my first thought of course was "Wow, you really could use some yoga." And then I wished this reviewer and I could have a conversation. Because I agreed with him on some level—yoga isn't *all* that one needs. I have seen many yogis act in very un-yogic ways and fall apart in spite of their yoga practice. People turn to many things, and it's important to have support beyond the yoga. The reason that I write about yoga is not because I have reached "enlightenment." I doubt I ever will. That's not the goal. I write about yoga because I have seen what it can do for the kids I teach.

When my own kids were in preschool, I decided that I was going to teach them how to meditate. I was teaching other kids in school how to practice mindfulness and meditation and do yoga, and

I wanted my own kids to have the tools to start caring for themselves in ways that I'd never been able to as a kid. Surely, if I was doing this for a living in schools, I could teach my own kids, right?

I imagined that meditation would be a great way for my kids to wind down after school and I thought it would be something special we could do together. I knew, in the beginning, that it wouldn't last for more than five minutes at first, and that was fine. But I assumed the more we did it together, the longer our "sessions" would be. I set up an altar with fun items to get them interested. I had crystals and statues and pictures of the kids. I had chimes and a singing bowl, and I invited each of them to put something special on our family altar. I bought fun meditation cushions with stars and planets on them because it's all about the accessories, after all. I had our meditation spot tricked out. I knew what this practice did for me—calming my mind, grounding me when I felt untethered, helping me to be present and accept my emotions, even if those emotions were anger, irritation, or anxiety. Naturally, I expected that yoga would do all of these things for my children. I was so excited to share this important self-care skill with my kids, which they would take with them into their stress-free futures, and of course, they would have me to thank for it. Oh, the ego is so interesting.

Our first meditation sessions together *were* pretty magical. They loved their cushions and held the crystals. Together, we listened to our breath, we set a timer, and with some minimal wiggles and giggles we did it! They were able to sit still until they heard the sound of the singing bowl, which meant that "class" was over. We kept this up for a few blissful weeks. Sometimes we would light a candle and practice single-pointed focus and that was fun albeit slightly scary because well . . . fire. But soon, I found myself struggling to get them to join me for our "quiet" time, which turned out not to be so quiet. In fact, it became a total sh*t show. They were busy or bouncy and resistant. Eventually, it felt like I was forcing them into something they didn't want to do, and I gave up. Occasionally they would join me again on their own, but I couldn't cajole them into a regular practice. And suddenly, there I was again in a place of self-loathing and failure. What was wrong with me? Why could I teach this to strangers' kids but not to my own?

My yoga and mindfulness practices have saved me so many times through the years. They have given me a way out of destructive thought patterns, a way to connect with myself and my breath, and a chance to practice letting go. That first class my friend dragged me to, the one where I tried to hide in my baggy clothes, changed everything for me. It was the first time I felt safe and grounded. It was the first break I got from my brain. Over time I got better at the poses and stronger in my mind and body and began building my toolbox. Filling it with resilience, empathy, presence. Something in me opened and at the same time something softened, and I joined a community of others wanting to fill their own toolboxes.

I so badly wanted all of this for my kids. Yoga and meditation couldn't solve it all, as that reviewer had not-so-kindly pointed out, but I deeply believed that these practices could help my kids as they had helped me. But of course, best-laid plans. My kids had zero interest in meditating with me. Practicing yoga together was always challenging and never as I envisioned, no matter how much fun I tried to make it, encouraging them to bark while in downward-dog pose or to slither across the mat like a snake. They only did it when they had to, like when I was teaching yoga to their preschool class and there was no escape, or later, when they were middle schoolers and I convinced them to participate as a favor in one of my studio classes because I needed more bodies. But otherwise, no.

First, I was hurt. This was a rejection of me. Then, I was sure there would be something missing in their lives without yoga— maybe a connection to their inner selves, a way to manage their emotions, or a greater sense of spirituality. And it was all my fault because I couldn't find a way to teach them. Ultimately, those were thoughts and feelings I had to sit with and be curious about and let pass. I had to find a way to accept their decision. Still, I wondered how they would learn to be present in their lives. I was so caught up in this way of thinking that I wasn't seeing how they could play in a pile of leaves forever or how they could lie in the grass and notice everything about an insect. Or how on a walk they would stop and look up at the sky. It took a while, but eventually, my kids pulled me out of the rigidity of my seated meditations, and they forced me to recognize that there are many ways to be present in our lives. Kids do this naturally. They already knew. They had options that didn't require teaching. I had options too, but I had forgotten them.

So, I let them be. I finally stopped projecting and assuming, and instead, I started paying attention. I watched and I saw something beautiful happening. It wasn't that they didn't get swept up in their emotions or that they didn't have highs and lows—of course they did. But I began to see that they had found their own ways of being present. As the kids got older and became teenagers, and life threw more at them, I watched them take it all on. I was there, ready to jump in again with *my* tools and *my* thoughts and *my* practices, which still worked for me. But they had found their own meditations.

One on the water, surfing. Waiting patiently for a wave. Breathing with the rhythm of the water. Noticing the temperature, the fish, the seaweed, the colors. The horizon. And then catching the wave and finding balance on the board, followed by the ride, the crash, the tumble. On repeat like a toddler's favorite storybook, asked to be read "again." Nowhere else but right there.

One on the floor, surrounded by paints and canvas and brushes. Focused on each stroke. Colors, patterns, shapes, textures. Not thinking about the end result, only the process. Experimenting and exploring. Nowhere else but right there.

One on the field. Paying attention to the turf, the play, the ball. The drills. The movement of feet. No thought of crowds and noise except the sound of a ball whooshing through the air. The catch. The run. The speed. Muscles working. Nowhere else but right there.

They don't have to explain any of this to me. I see it. The more I pay attention, the more I notice the many moments in which they are fully present, aware, engaged. I see them breathing deeply, setting boundaries, finding ways to care for themselves. When they feel untethered and overwhelmed, they can tap into the feelings, the breath, the memory, and ground themselves. This is their meditation. In the end, that is all I want for them, and they found it all on their own.

So, to that reviewer, I will keep sharing what I know with love and enthusiasm. I will not assume that my practice is everyone's cure-all or path to enlightenment. Instead, I will hope that the people in my life—my children, my students, my readers—will discover their own way of being fully in the here and now. And I will celebrate the path they take to get there.

As I reconnect to my breath,
I am present.

CHAPTER 5

INSIDE AND OUTSIDE THINGS

Recently my shower door came off its hinges and stopped closing all the way. Every time I showered, water pooled under the door on the floor, ultimately dripping from the second floor, through the ceiling to the first floor, causing damage above and below. The upside was I had insurance that allowed for the renovation. And for a minute, there was a silver lining. But then came the other flood of total anxiety as decorating and design are not my strong suits and I have never been able to imagine what an empty room or one that needs redoing could or should look like. I look at a space and I see a space.

After my mental flood, all I could think about was the time I would have to spend without a functioning bathroom, that I would have to share a bathroom with my teenagers, and how inconvenient, gross (teenagers), and stressful the whole thing would be. I called my mother and together we went to pick out tiles and fixtures and all that jazz. At the showroom I was totally overwhelmed by the choices and colors. Trying to imagine the finished space and what would fit where was just too much. I blame this inability to look at shapes and see how they will fit together on my high school geometry teacher. He was terrible and weirdly inappropriate (today he would most likely have been swiftly removed from his position). He would throw me out of class when I wore my "all the rage" jeans with holes in them (you can imagine the comments he made) so naturally I wore them almost every day and basically was never in class. I feel like I never developed a sense of spatial relationships or measurements as a result and at the same time I cultivated my terrible math phobia that still infiltrates my life.

At the showroom I tried to be a big girl and show my mom that as an adult I was no longer completely useless when it came to these things. But I was still completely useless. Thankfully, I was saved by a phone call that required my full attention and in the five minutes I was gone my mother had worked her magic. She had everything chosen and it was exactly what I wanted without me even knowing what I wanted. I have always seen this as my mother's superpower. She can make things look beautiful. This is how she's always been.

In early fall, over a year into the pandemic, my mother and I were walking our dogs along the beach. We had been meeting in this same spot to walk our dogs almost every day since the start of summer. I don't know why, but each time we meet I am struck by the differences between the two of us and our two dogs. The dogs are both Coton de Tulears and they come from the same breeder in California, so most likely they are related. They are both white and small and from the same gene pool, but otherwise they could not be more different.

My mom's dog, Beatrice (or Bea, as we call her), is female and a year or two younger than my dog, Gizmo. Bea has a sweet, soft face, which she tilts slightly when you speak to her as though she is very interested in what you have to say. My mother drops all prepositions when conversing with Bea in a kind of irritating baby talk. The dog's hair (not fur) always looks as though she is fresh from the groomer, and she smells of perfumy powder. Bea wears a rotation of outfits for her walks, depending on the season, and her harness is stitched with her full name, BEATRICE, in big, bold lettering. As soon as they get to the beach, my mother lets Bea off her leash, and she never strays far. As gentle as she looks, when other dogs arrive, my mother has to warn them of Bea's temperament and the likelihood she will attack no matter their size.

Gizmo, on the other hand, is not delicate. He has a big fluffy face and kind eyes and always looks like he's had a rough day. He smells terrible due to the tartar on his teeth that we can't seem to get rid of no matter how many times he goes to the doggie dentist. Although he too goes to the groomer, his hair is always unkempt. His harness never seems to fit properly and his tattered leash remains attached during our walks, as otherwise he will not stay close and would surely wander off into the dunes. But Gizmo is forever happy, jolly even. He skips along the water's edge, he loves other dogs, and he never bites or growls but just wants to meet and greet everyone. If I had to warn any nearby dog owner about Gizmo's behavior it would be to say that if you, human or dog, have any food, he will most likely try to take it from you in a very friendly way. My ex-husband, Evan, hates Gizmo and ignores him whenever he visits the house; I think because he sees Gizmo as his replacement. I got Gizmo just months after my ex moved out, so he may be right.

My mother and I are as different from one another as our dogs. Like Bea, my mother always has on a chic outfit befitting the season. Although pandemic fashion has been mostly exercise clothing or athleisure wear, hers is still put together and looks as though she actually put some thought into it. Her hair is simple but stylish and her subtle makeup is fresh and lovely. Someone once described my mother to me as being youthful, and that is right. She has an energy about her that keeps her young even as she hits her late seventies.

I, on the other hand, typically dress like a teenager who has picked her nearest and cleanest-smelling clothes from the floor to wear, whether they match or not. In the pandemic my hair has gotten too long, and while I do love my long, thick hair, it has turned ropy instead of wavy and it's always a bit knotted. I never wear makeup and frankly wouldn't know how to apply it without feeling like I was playing dress-up. Perhaps I should be wearing some at this point in my life, but I can't be bothered to learn. I walk the beach barefoot even though it's a bit chilly. If I could be without shoes all year long that would make me very happy. In my early twenties I wore nothing but heels and somehow was able to walk, run, and dance in them as though they were sneakers, but now I prefer a good pedicure and free feet. A good pedicure is something my mother and I always have had in common. Beneath her clean sneakers I know she has freshly painted toes just like me.

These differences between us are not new. When I was a child, my mother was always the one who kept up appearances. She married my father when they were very young, and more sophisticated than he was, she was determined to show him her world and how to fit into it. Hers was a world of culture and beauty and she introduced that world to me and my brother too. She gave us books and took us to French films that we were much too young for, and she would cover our eyes whenever there was a sex scene (which of course only made us more interested in watching). She was a fabulous cook, and when she was home she made us beautiful meals. When she took us shopping for school clothes, she instructed the salespeople to dress us up so we wouldn't "look like drug addicts" (which now of course feels incredibly offensive on many levels). She decorated our homes and even when we couldn't afford fancy things, always knowing how to take something secondhand and make it look brand-new.

Appearances were important. Outside was more important than inside, more important than me and my brother, or so it seemed. It wasn't that we didn't enjoy time with her. She loved fun and experiences and embraced life. We went to the theater, we took trips, we swam at the beach, went shopping, played games and did puzzles by candlelight when a hurricane caused a blackout. We had dinners outdoors in the summer and went sledding in the winter. She made all of it happen. She was the one who made sure that she and my dad had a social life and that they traveled the world. She always had interesting and creative jobs. She also had deep friendships. She seemed to be so open and free and kind with her friends. I longed for her to be just as at ease with me. But I was too emotional, and there was too much need, so instead she pulled away, shut down, or disappeared.

My mother did not seem to relish being a mother. Unlike my father, who was unpredictable and prone to explosive anger, my mother kept an emotional distance. Mothering wasn't what filled her soul. Work, travel, my father, friends, a social life—these things made her feel alive. I could see it in her being. It was clear. For her, things on the outside could easily be fixed, spruced up, and made to look good. Things on the inside were too much work, ugly and messy. And I was filled with inside things.

When I was a teenager, my mother opened a tabletop store called Kitchen Classics out where we usually spent our summers, once again pulling her away from us and our lives in the city. My father commuted back and forth to Manhattan for work and, used to being on our own, my brother and I continued living in our city apartment to go to school, only going out to visit on the occasional weekend and in summer. My mother's store was filled with gorgeous linens, dishes, and flatware from places like Paris and Italy and all kinds of cookware. There were coffee beans sold by the pound, freshly ground while you waited. There was every kind of kitchen gadget one could imagine. The space smelled of fresh-cut flowers or pine needles, depending on the time of year, and of French roast or an exotic spice. Her inventory was often used for photo shoots in cookbooks or food magazines. It was in fact a welcoming and inviting shop with a little something for everyone. She put her heart and soul into this place, and you could feel it. Almost fifteen years after its closing people still stop her on the street to say they miss her store. It was her outlet to focus on beautiful things. And like I've said, she had a gift.

Some summers I worked grudgingly behind the register. I needed a job and loved spending my free time at the beach, and her store gave me that opportunity. But Kitchen Classics was not my scene and being with my mother in a small space was never easy. I'm not even sure why she let me work there. Surely she recognized how bumpy our relationship was, and it's not like I knew or cared about table linens. Maybe she was trying to let me into her world or maybe she just needed summer help and I needed to work. But I was resentful. She cared so much about these precious, beautiful, material things. They were interesting to her and worthy of her attention. I was not. I was moody and anxious and struggling with myself. I didn't fit in. We clashed and more than once she fired me or I quit.

In my twenties, after some time on my own living in New York City and working in places quite the opposite of my mother's store, the job I'd had ended and I needed to figure out my next move. My mother allowed me once again to try working for her and agreed to let me temporarily stay at my parents' beach house. At this point, I knew myself better. I understood the limits of our relationship and I was able to keep my own emotional distance. This time I was able to pick and choose pieces of myself to show her. I knew what was too difficult and unattractive and I knew what was easy for her. This time I watched her in her element, engaging with beautiful things and the people who wanted to buy them, and I fully embraced it. I decided to try to learn about her world instead of rejecting it, which gave me a way in. When she noticed I was interested, she started taking me with her on these absolutely fabulous and over-the-top buying trips to Paris, teaching me about dishes and linens and all things tabletop and how to both use them and choose them for the store. On these trips, we were good. How could we not be? We were in France, where everything was beautiful, and I started to understand her just a little bit better in between gift shows and over shared plates of cheese and cups of café au lait. We were figuring out how to make it work, make us work.

Eventually, I figured out my own path and went back to college to become a teacher, I met a man who I would marry (and divorce), and my summer place became my permanent place. I started to make a life. And as my parents got older, they too made this their home base and their visits back to Manhattan became less frequent. We lived minutes away from one another and my mother and I had figured out how to connect on the surface. We traveled, we decorated the tiny home I shared with Evan, we even planned my wedding together. Any feelings that were too much or too ugly were kept out of it. I had friends and a partner for that. I had a therapist for that. But there was always a part of me that wanted my mother for that. During this time, my mother's best friend contracted AIDS and was dying. He was her decorator from long ago and they had bonded over furniture and wallpaper, but the relationship got deeper as time went on and when he got sick my mother didn't pull away. She was there, caring for him, loving him, and being there with his pain and her own until he was gone. I knew she was capable of emotions that were hard and there was nothing pretty about AIDS or the way in which her friend slowly died. Nothing to be spruced up or cleaned up. But this wasn't a side she was willing to share with her children.

It wasn't until I decided to have children of my own that something shifted. I knew that I would be a different kind of mother than she had been. I couldn't wait to be there for all of the messy emotions and issues that came with children (even though I had no clue what was in store). I needed that to fill *my* soul. I was going to be completely and utterly attached. But what I didn't expect was that my mother would become attached too. As soon as it became clear that

I was having trouble becoming pregnant, and that I was going to try IVF, she was there by my side. She was with me for every appointment at the fertility clinic and every OB-GYN appointment. She was there for the shots and the struggles and the feelings. She saw that my marriage was messy, and I needed a partner, and that is who she became. This was major inside stuff, and she didn't shy away from it. I didn't ask why, and I didn't reject this sudden attention. I soaked it all in.

Once my kids were born, she was immediately in love with them. Only later would I learn that while I was lucky enough to be enjoying everything about being pregnant, she was having literal panic attacks worrying about their safety in utero. Once they entered the world, the deep love and connection she had for my kids became abundantly clear. As with all babies they were full of needs and demands, the kind she didn't want to take on with her own children. But she took them on as their grandma.

My kids have only experienced my mother as the supportive, loving, funny, smart, and very chic grandma who enjoys her cocktails at the end of the day. They know how to win her over when they want something I can't afford or something I might say no to, and she is putty in their hands. She does the beautiful things with them—the trips, the shopping, the theater—because these are the things that are her gifts. They each love going away with her because she is always up for an adventure, and she is an incredibly "chill" traveler as my son says (unlike me). No matter how down and dirty they get on these trips, she will also make sure that each day ends in a gorgeous hotel where everyone can rest and relax. My mother has been all over the world, making friends wherever she goes and absorbing life in different cultures and places, filling her soul. She is fearless and fully present when she travels just as she is fully present as a grandmother.

She does not turn away from the hard things with my kids. When Jacob's OCD showed up, she jumped right in to help in any way she could. When Jesse changed their pronouns, she started using them without needing an explanation and without her view of Jesse changing even a little. When Ben wanted to pursue his dream of going to boarding school to play football, she was there to help make it happen. When he was badly injured and feeling down on himself, she was there too. My kids get the best of her.

Why is it so easy for her to love my kids? Why wasn't she able to be that way with me? They are messy and emotional. They are needy and demanding. What's different? Was it my fault?

My mother was young when she had me and my brother. She did what she thought the world expected of her. But there was no glamour in having children. She felt deprived, robbed of a life of exploration and adventure. Her childhood home had been cold and formal, and she longed for freedom. Kids had interfered, depriving her of that adventure. Kids took an emotional toll. Kids created pain and discomfort and worry. That wasn't what she'd wanted. Attachment meant time, investment, and a loss of herself and those were things she couldn't bear. So, she detached.

I was the opposite. I longed for connection with my kids. I wanted to show myself and I wanted to show her that I was different. I thought I was making a conscious choice to express my deep feelings for my children, but it wasn't entirely conscious. It seemed on a cellular level that it was near impossible for me to keep my emotions *out* of parenting. Every time my kids experience a disappointment or a major setback, I am the one who feels sick. It's like their pain goes right to my belly and I am hit with waves of nausea. Somehow, they seem to miraculously rebound, whereas I hang on and hold tight to whatever they have experienced, reliving it for them and wishing that I could turn back the clock and prevent whatever just happened. It's as if I think that if I just reopen that rejection letter or replay the soul-crushing scenario in my head enough times, I can change it. But, of course, I can't.

I work on keeping all of this to myself and I try with all my might not to project my anxiety onto them. I try to create a space for them to talk or to just deal in their own way. I know they must suffer to learn and grow. I know things won't always go their way. I know this is life. But inside, it is crushing for me to see them in any sort of discomfort. Am I too connected? Too invested? Too enmeshed? Maybe. But honestly, I don't know how to be any other way.

By choosing to be there for my children, her grandchildren, my mother was also going to have to see me fall apart with worry, and care and love deeply. I wouldn't be able to shut it off for her sake and I didn't want to. But this was never a demand she made. In fact, she too became completely enmeshed. She stayed with me through the sleepless nights and the tears and the messes. She was in it. When problems got bigger and feelings were more complex, she didn't pull away and shut down. And in my most painful parenting moments, I began to understand her. It wasn't me. This parenting thing is just *hard*, and she had needed to disconnect to survive. In this safe space of mothering and grandmothering, I learned that she too was full of inside things.

Today, when we walk along the beach together, maybe it is the soft sand or the sound of water rippling gently on the shore, but we are both open and at ease. I can ask questions and hear things that would have once wounded me. She can absorb and express the feelings she has carried with her. Maybe a global pandemic and getting older have given us reasons to say it all and not hold back. Maybe these children we love are the motivation. Maybe we are just finally brave enough to be vulnerable.

I stop to let Gizmo poop for the third time as my mother walks ahead. She pauses for a moment and looks longingly at the beautiful houses overlooking the beach. I know she is wishing my father was still alive and that they were back together in their own beautiful beach house. I can see her body slump slightly and the sadness in her face that for a moment overtakes her.

Suddenly, as if she knows she is being watched, she straightens and calls for Bea, handing her the treats she keeps in the pocket of her designer jacket. The two of them look like a photo in a magazine, Bea and Mom, perfectly styled with a bright blue sky and the soft green bay water as backdrop. And here I am with my messy, pooping dog and my mismatched clothes, hair getting knottier with each gust of wind, wondering what my kids are doing at home without me, and thinking about how, soon, they will be off living their lives without me. I feel myself slump slightly with sadness. But then, just like my mom, I pull it together. I catch up to her and we walk, grandmother and mother, mother and mother, mother and daughter.

The entirety of
my being is beautiful.

CHAPTER 6

LIVE FREE

I have a recurring dream that starts with me in the car driving into Manhattan and approaching the Midtown Tunnel. I am feeling happy because I know that I am headed into the city, and that feels like going home. Ahead of me, I can see that the cars inside the tunnel are at a standstill. As I slowly pull up to the entrance, I can make out the rear of a big yellow school bus in the left lane. A traffic cop appears and directs me into the right lane, telling me to pull up next to the bus. I say, "Are you sure? Is it safe? It looks like no one is moving." But just as she might in real life, the traffic cop has no response and no patience for me and just keeps waving me forward. I pull into the tunnel and sidle up next to the yellow school bus, which I notice has no windows and I can't see if anyone is inside. I inch further forward and then stop. Suddenly, I realize that we are all going nowhere . . . ever. I am forever stuck, smooshed between the side of the yellow bus and the wall. There is no backing up and no going forward and this is how I am going to die, in the Midtown Tunnel between a bus and a wall.

Every time, I jerk awake, terrified, heart pounding and gasping for breath. Instantly, I start thanking everyone and everything that it was only a dream. I am sure that someone out there could interpret this dream on a deeper level, but my takeaway is that somewhere in my psyche I feel stuck, or I am worried about getting stuck, and perhaps I am afraid I will die from the stuck-ness.

This past year, my sixteen-year-old, Jesse, called me into their room to have a chat. I always know when my kids have something significant to be discussed. It's in the tone of their voices and the way they say "Can you come here? I need to ask you something." I always give myself a little pep talk *before* these chats with my kids. Whatever the situation is, I know we will work it out, and if I have to say "no" or tell them something they don't want to hear, then so be it.

I went into Jesse's room and plopped myself on the floor with a bit of a forced cheerful expression.

"What's up?" I asked, not entirely ready for what would come next.

"Mom. I want to talk about top surgery."

Jesse had come out as transgender earlier that year, and I'd known this discussion might be on the horizon. Jesse was struggling to find comfort in their body and their gender. I had watched this struggle and done my best to offer support without too much hovering: always letting them stay home from school on days when the dysphoria was unbearable, buying the binders and clothing that they needed to feel somewhat better, and trying to show them how much they were enough and how much they were loved. But for some reason I was caught off guard by Jesse's mention of surgery. I shouldn't have been. I had been learning about gender-affirming surgeries and how important they can be for mental health. But this felt big. And fast. And I couldn't help but wonder if Jesse was too young to make this decision. I guess I'd figured we would have more time before this came up. I still had more of my own work to do.

Despite my pre-discussion breathing and pep talk, in the moment, I messed it all up. Instead of giving Jesse what they needed, I reacted like a scared mom or a scared little girl. The look on my face was one of fear. Jesse could see it right away. I didn't pause or listen or think about my response. I just rode the wave of emotion that welled up inside of me the minute I heard "top surgery." Despite my years of practicing mindfulness and the unquantifiable amount of love I have for Jesse, I panicked. The thoughts in my head were:

Was this it? Would the Jesse I had known their whole life be gone forever?

What if Jesse regretted the decision?

Surgery is dangerous!

I heard myself saying the last two of these things out loud, instead of keeping them inside. I rambled on about surgery being unsafe and I challenged their readiness to make such a big decision. I brought up cost and the potential what-ifs. I didn't ask how they were feeling or if they had worries or concerns. I made it about my fears. My tone and my energy and my panicked look said even more than words ever could. Jesse realized there was no conversation to be had, no calm, no softness. They threw me out of their room, yelling that I was acting like a terrible person and that they couldn't talk to me before slamming the door. Jesse was right of course. I was obviously not in a place to be able to talk about anything. I returned to my own room and sat with myself, feeling like a jerk.

Earlier that year, when Jesse had first told me they were trans, I knew there would be a lot to come as they embraced who they were and tried to navigate this new outward, but not so new inward, experience. I wanted so badly to understand everything so that I could be supportive and not mess it up. I was lucky enough to have a close friend to turn to whose child was assigned female at birth and who at twenty-one had told his mother that he was, in fact, male. Then came the testosterone and subsequent surgeries, and he is now happier than he has ever been. This was a process and not without struggles, but in the end, it was beautiful to see him finally safe and supported as his true self.

My friend told me that when her son first shared that he was male, she thought about it for just a minute, and then said to herself, "Well, that makes perfect sense." It was instantly clear to her that this was and had always been so. But with Jesse, it had not been so clear to me. I knew they were probably queer from a very young age. (Just a disclaimer: the terms, name, and pronouns I am using when talking about Jesse are the ones of their choosing, not ones I have assumed fit them best.) Looking back, it's hard to articulate how I knew, I just did. When my kids were little, their father and I made a concerted effort not to reinforce traditional gender constructs with them. We didn't say things like "*This* is only for girls or boys." Everything was for everyone. They all wore and played with whatever spoke to them. Jesse went through a period in which they loved sparkles and pink and princesses, and so did their brothers. However, there is no way to shut out the influence of the outside world. I am sure that despite our best efforts, stereotypes and limitations and definitions trickled in.

When Jesse came out to me as queer at fourteen, it wasn't a surprise. In fact, it almost felt unnecessary for them to state. Sometimes, in my online searches for more information on LBGTQ+ experiences, I would come across YouTube videos posted mostly by teenagers of themselves coming out to their parents. In these videos, the parents were always accepting and loving and comforted their child as the child sobbed with relief. In reality, we know that there are so many situations that don't end happily: kids who have to hide who they are, or when they do come out, they get kicked out of their homes and shamed and shunned by family, churches, and communities. Whenever I watched one of these happier videos, I would end up sobbing along with the kids and families on-screen and then I would go give each of my kids a whole speech about how they should never be afraid to tell me anything to which they would say "I know, Mooooomm."

Jesse's coming out to me began with a text.

Jesse: I have to tell you something, but I don't want to talk about it after.
Me: (thinking I knew exactly what was coming) Okay
Jesse: I am Bi
Me: (close enough) Okay
Jesse: Okay

Then, two hours later:

Jesse: I think I want to talk about it.
Me: Okay

And so, we talked about it. Jesse knew I would be supportive
and happy for them that they were discovering who they were. This
wasn't a case of "I love you no matter what." There was nothing here
that I had to love Jesse in spite of. It was what it was. It didn't alter a
single thing about my love and feelings for Jesse. And I was relieved
they finally wanted to talk.

We sat down in their room, and Jesse explained to me that their
stress surrounding whether or not to talk further about coming out
wasn't about feeling accepted or not. It was about worry over having
boxed themselves in with a label by saying they were bi. This label
didn't capture the full spectrum of who they were, Jesse explained.
They wanted to clarify that, in fact, they were not entirely sure that
bi was accurate. They were attracted to girls and boys, but they also
felt in conflict with the gender assigned to them at birth. They often
felt more boy than girl but also, like both, and also like neither. They
weren't sure how I would handle *that*, and they didn't know how to
really refer to themselves, but they wanted to be transparent and open
and share. They needed to talk it through. All I could do was listen.
I couldn't direct them one way or the other, as it obviously wasn't a
choice. I could only be there to love and honor and support.

A year later, when they came out as transgender/nonbinary, it
was more of a statement in passing from Jesse, and I was again the
one who wanted to talk. I had questions! But instead of imposing my
ignorance on Jesse, I ordered and read all the recommended books.
I started following transgender influencers on social media and

paying attention in a way I should have been all along. I tried to learn everything I could about what Jesse might be experiencing. I learned about their gender dysphoria and the terrible discomfort and burden of being in a body that didn't fit their gender identity versus body dysmorphia (which is what I suffer from). I learned about pronouns and listened to advice about how to handle the inevitable mistakes of someone using the wrong ones. I thought I was ready for more exploration and conversation whenever they were ready. But I still had a lot to unpack and my own internal bias that I wasn't even aware of and would need to confront.

Things were changing quickly with Jesse. For example, they used to love makeup. It was an artistic outlet, and whenever they felt down, they would re-create some amazing drag or exaggerated complicated look. I was in awe. I have never worn, nor do I know how to wear makeup, let alone do contouring. Jesse was always collecting different makeup palettes and brushes and the tools any professional makeup artist might use. Then, all of that abruptly ended. No more makeup and soon all the skirts and dresses were in a donation pile and everything that might be considered overtly feminine was rejected. And it was all OK.

One evening, Jesse emerged from the bathroom with a moustache. It was a real moustache, as we are a dark-haired family who can easily grow a little 'stache if we are not paying attention. Jesse had made theirs a bit darker and more prominent with the help of some eyeliner and it looked very authentic. However, this was an incredibly jarring moment for me. They asked proudly, "What do you think of my moustache?" Oh God, I knew this was a moment in which I could either lose trust and really blow it or an opportunity to show my support. Everything in me hated that moustache. I had learned from a young age that facial hair, body hair in general, was not something a girl should have/want/keep. The shaving and waxing started early for me, and to this day I always carry a tweezer with me in case that stray beard hair appears and needs immediate plucking. When I saw Jesse standing proudly in front of me with a moustache, those thoughts came back to me. I had *said* I was cool with Jesse's gender expression, but when faced with it, I was clearly holding onto the idea of Jesse as a girl and the "rules" that went along with that. It was all I could do not to plead with them to wax it off ASAP! But that was about me, not them.

Me: deep breath

Me: another deep breath

Me: yet another deep breath

(Pause)

Me, finally: You know, I am a little challenged by your moustache as I am so used to waxing my whole face. But if you love it then that is what counts. (Again, approaching Jesse as though they were a girl, from the perspective of another girl who was taught that facial hair was not OK. My own issues. My own ideas. My own obvious misunderstanding of a nonbinary experience. In retrospect if I had been as without bias as I had ignorantly claimed my response would have been different and not full of my own cis-angst.)

Jesse: I LOVE IT!

Soon after the moustache, Jesse told me they wanted to use different pronouns (they/them) and use a different name that felt more like them: Jesse. I supported all of this, of course, but then came more feelings. Ones that I had not been fully aware were buried deep down. There was something about that moustache that had given me a little ache for the first time. I think because it was such a visible departure from the Jesse I had been choosing to see for the last sixteen years through my narrow cisgender lens. This was despite the fact that Jesse had explained to me that they had never been comfortable as that person. When my boys first started showing off their barely visible moustaches, it would never have crossed my mind that this was not the way it should be. By contrast, before Jesse had come out, I had taught them how to shave their legs and armpits, and we'd gone for eyebrow and lip waxes together. Again, through my cisgender lens I'd just thought that was what girls do. It's what I had been brought up to believe girls were *supposed* to do. But now suddenly I realized that I had been boxing Jesse in, making assumptions not only about their gender identity but also what was "required" within that assumed gender. Instead of creating an environment for Jesse in which they felt free to choose, free to be, which I had claimed was so important to me as a parent, I was doing the opposite. I was stuck in an antiquated and frankly repressive way of thinking, and I found myself wondering how I'd ended up there.

I have always thought of myself as an ally, as an open, loving, accepting person. I grew up in the West Village in the seventies and eighties and queer culture was nothing new and had been part of my daily life. It made perfect sense to me that out of my three kids, at least one would be gay. The terms trans and nonbinary were a bit new to me. Looking back, I had known and loved many trans people in my life, but the term wasn't in my vernacular. I had not witnessed the actual process or pain or joy in my friends becoming their true selves. I just knew them and loved them as who they were and stood up for and by them the best way I knew how.

Now, I was not only a witness to this process as I watched my child change, but I was also part of it. My reactions and support were integral to their story. And that was incredibly scary. I didn't want to screw it up. When I heard the words "top surgery," I became selfishly fixated on my ideas of Jesse's old self-expression. Stuck in what was. Not able to move and go with the flow.

I have felt stuck many times throughout my life. Sitting in discomfort. Thinking this feeling would be forever. The discomfort of my childhood; stuck in a cycle of believing I was a disappointment and worth nothing. The discomfort of my marriage; stuck in a feeling of despair and thinking this would always be my relationship. The discomfort of my body; never being at ease with it, feeling like I would always be working to make it better.

But I had also gotten unstuck. I had also felt free.

When I was in my late teens and early twenties, I was a club kid in NYC. Living in my first apartment on the Upper West Side, I had a job I loved, I was going to yoga, and I had cultivated a family I had chosen versus the one I had grown up with. Within this family were DJs, bankers, students, restaurant owners, drug dealers, music execs, wannabe artists, up-and-coming rappers, some "kids" without jobs and some with. We were Jewish, Dominican, Black, Asian, Puerto Rican, White, and everything else you could think of. We loved each other. We saw each other. We met each night at some spot downtown in the early evening (except on Fridays and Saturdays, as those were "bridge and tunnel" nights, meaning the tourists and frat boys and not real New Yorkers were out). We would eat, hang out, just be together, until it was time to hit the club. We mostly went to Nell's on 14th Street, and sometimes an after-hours club in Alphabet City. There were no lines for us or velvet ropes holding us back. We knew bouncers and club owners and just slid right in. We mingled with celebrities and young A and R people from different record labels looking for new talent. We were all there for the house music that would send us into a trance. We were there for the connection. There was no judgment, only love. We saw each other and accepted each other. I have never felt more like my true self than when we were together. This family I had become a part of was where I felt safe.

They were not questioning my love interests, my jobs, my choices. They were giving me space to be me and support when I needed it. It was all I needed to be free. Ultimately there were marriages and moves, deaths and jobs that took us away from each other. The critical words from my past crept back in. And that freedom was lost in my own marriage and motherhood and the struggle to love myself again.

I have shared bits and pieces of this time in my life with my kids as they have gotten older. They have met some of my "family" who are still in my life. They know about the music and the rappers who would battle outside the club on any given night. I have managed to pass on an appreciation for nineties hip-hop and they have seen me go into a dancing trance to house music (which I am sure is embarrassing for them, but I don't care). But there are some things I will never tell. Some stories are for me alone. What I do tell my kids is that this was a time when I was totally myself and even though it didn't last forever, it was amazing. It is something I can think back to when I feel stuck and when discomfort seems permanent. The memory of those days, that feeling of freedom, helps me to move forward and to find it within myself again and again. My wish for my kids is that they too will discover this kind of freedom in their lives, even if it is brief. I hope it becomes something they can think back on, as a reminder that stuck-ness—in a thought pattern, a behavior, or a feeling—is temporary, and freedom is possible.

I had imagined that one day my kids would have similar experiences, ones that gave them a sense of freedom that they could hold onto as the responsibilities of adulthood set in. However, I could see that for Jesse, finding freedom wouldn't be about letting loose in a nightclub or finding themselves through travel—though I hope they will do those things. For Jesse, it was more complicated, and it wasn't going to be so fleeting. This was about getting to be who they truly are.

A few hours after throwing me out of their room following my disappointing (to say the least) reaction to the top-surgery announcement, Jesse came into my room wanting to talk. I was so relieved. It should have been me coming to them and not the other way around. Instead, they were comforting me when they were the one who should have been comforted. Jesse told me they loved me, and they understood my fears. They had fears of their own. But they needed me, and they needed to be able to have a real conversation with me, because *they* were feeling stuck. They actually used the word "stuck." Jesse explained that they needed to be able to say out loud what they felt inside. They didn't want unsolicited opinions or advice from me. They needed me to listen. They needed me to be there even if I was uncomfortable or afraid. In that moment, I understood. It was a time for *me* to get unstuck. I needed and wanted to be their safe space. I wanted our relationship to be different from the one I had with my own parents at their age. I hadn't felt the freedom to be who I was without judgment. I wanted them to experience the feeling of being totally themselves as I had with my club "family." I wanted to be that someone they could turn to without having to explain or justify their choices. They were going to face so much of that in the outside world, and they already had.

This time, Jesse's wisdom, openness, their light and love became the lifeline that pulled both of us out of the quicksand. I am eternally grateful to them for that, and I am sorry that I wasn't able to be the one to pull us out. I thought of the freedom I had experienced and that I wanted for my children, for my Jesse. If I am to be a part of their freedom, I know I must be willing to confront my own biases, to unpack my own issues, to push back against inaccurate and antiquated belief systems. I must keep noticing where I am still stuck, and I must do the work. And this is work that I so want to do. This is the work I am committed to doing. Jesse, the amazing, courageous, beautiful soul that I have the privilege of mothering, has given me a second chance. I won't waste it, Jesse. I will do better.

I haven't had my Midtown Tunnel dream for a while. I believe I can thank Jesse for that, for pushing me past the feeling that I might die from being permanently trapped, stifled by my stuck-ness, and bringing me to a place where I can choose to look at myself, at what I am holding onto, let go and move forward. Jesse showed me all of this even though they didn't have to, even though they might not have wanted to. As their journey continues and Jesse allows me in, I do worry because I know I will continue to make mistakes. I know I have more "undoing" to do. But I also know that I have been given an opportunity to stretch and grow and learn and I don't take any of that for granted. Maybe, if my dream does return, this time I will know better and choose a different route, one that leaves the unmoving bus and the darkness of the tunnel behind me. I will make a better choice, and I will find my way into that beautiful city where I have felt at home and free.

I am able to break the patterns,
do the work, and create
a safe space where truth
is honored, love exists, and
freedom is possible.

CHAPTER 7

ALREADY A HERO

The other night when Jacob had his crew of friends over, he sent me a text from his room (which is shouting distance from mine):

"Food, please!"

These days, this is what passes for communication, even when we are in the same house. Entering Jacob's room is only done via invitation, as if I am a vampire. I am always excited to be summoned, even if I act otherwise. As my kids have grown, my duties as a mom have shifted. It's no longer MOMMMMEEEEE every thirty seconds. Today I am most useful to them as driver, chef, one-woman clean-up crew, and appointment scheduler. Otherwise, it's best to remain out of sight. When I act outside of those functions, I'm likely to be referred to as "bruh" and told to "chill."

This shift in my role as mom to teenagers was abrupt, and I am still trying to figure out how to respect their boundaries and not let the fact that I miss my babies get in the way of appreciating them now. I have become a loving spectator, observing from a safe distance as my kids move through the world, waiting for my cue to join in, and trying not to lose it when the dishes and dirty clothes pile up behind the mostly closed doors of their rooms and then spill out into our shared living spaces.

That night as I brought food into Jacob's room, out of nowhere, he blurted out to his friends that I once fought off a mugger with three feet of a six-foot hero. I was totally shocked—not only that he remembered the story, but that he thought it was worthy of sharing, and in a non-sarcastic way. This is interacting with teenagers. The moments in which they talk to me about what is happening in their lives or include me in the conversation are rare and spontaneous. They always seem to catch me off guard. It will be a random moment of passing in the kitchen or a long car ride or a late night where we just happen to be in the same room at the same time. It's on their terms. And when it happens, I hold very still, afraid that any movement will scare them off. As they talk, I tell myself not to say too much or interject or interrupt unless specifically asked and just let their side of things flow like a stream of consciousness until it's over, all while making sure I show just the right amount of interest and respond in just the right way if a response is required. It can be the most thrilling and exhausting few minutes of my life.

My kids' friends are incredibly cool. They are stylish and unique and interesting. Some are athletes and skateboarders and artists. Some are tattooed. They are nonbinary and trans and pan and straight and everything in between. They all have empathy and compassion and deep thoughts and are also hot messes in their own teenage ways. They are sassy and savvy and I find myself wanting to flop down next to them and hang out and revisit my younger, cooler self and discuss life. But I resist the temptation, of course, because they only know me as a mom. So, when Jacob mentioned my hero incident, I momentarily froze, waiting for my instructions about what to do next. Do I laugh? Shrug? Say "Yep" and quickly exit the room?

His friends asked for details and after getting the nod of approval from Jacob, I told them the story of my ride home from a party in high school and how I had taken the remainder of a hero home. This was weird because I didn't eat heros and my plan was to toss it as soon as I got back to my parents' apartment. But I was being polite. I explained how I casually hailed a cab (hoping they would all feel impressed by the city girl in me) and how I had the hero lying on the seat to the left of me while I sat all the way on the right side of the back seat. We stopped in Midtown at a red light, and suddenly a man flung open the back door of the taxi, reaching in and grasping for my bag, which was tucked under my right arm. Between us was the hero. As I yelled

"Drive! Drive!" to the cabbie, I picked up my three feet of a six-foot hero filled with lunch meats and lettuce and mustard . . . the works, and I started swinging. I hit the man enough times that he couldn't get to me, and thankfully the light changed and we took off.

I could feel myself bubbling with excitement as they listened. For a minute, I wasn't the old mom but the tough, street-smart, city kid I used to be. The one that could totally hang with them and fit right in. Then just as abruptly came "OK, Mom, thanks," my cue to go. I left and stood outside Jacob's door for a breath, feeling the glow of the fleeting spotlight.

Jacob and his friends seemed entertained by the image of me fending off an attacker with deli meats, but beyond that they weren't really interested in the nuances, ironies, and complexities of my hero story. So much about who I am is captured in this moment, starting with the fact that I took a hero home when I knew that I would never eat it, just to be polite. That right there is both the people pleaser and the disordered eater in me. The rigid dieter who constantly counted calories and never touched bread or lunch meat or really enjoyed food at all. Those parts of my personality seemingly more timid than courageous. Also, it's a little corny, but I love the double meaning of "hero" in this story—being my own hero with an actual hero, it's good stuff. But mostly, this story is a reminder for me of how I learned at a young age to protect myself with what I had. I didn't think of it as bravery, just survival.

When I was seven, while we were out, someone broke into my family's home in the West Village when we weren't home, stole a bunch of random things, and made a big mess. We had what I thought was an intricate alarm system made of wires wrapped around our front door, but the door was made of wood, so they just cut a hole right in the middle to bypass the alarm. We didn't have much to take, but it was terrifying enough to change the way I felt about my physical safety at home. We got a metal door after that with a police bolt, but I didn't feel much better. I no longer felt safe, but I didn't talk to anyone about it. In retrospect, it seems strange that we never talked as a family about the break-in. Perhaps my parents just thought that break-ins were normal, a risk that everyone takes living in a big city, or that they had remedied the situation with locks and bolts and doors and no conversation was necessary.

I decided to take things into my own hands, and in my bedroom I created an elaborate safety system that would alert me to an intruder in time to escape. My bedroom had two windows facing a public courtyard, one of which had an air-conditioning unit in it, so nobody could get in through that one. The other, above the fire escape, was the potential entry point. Underneath the sill next to my bed was an old-school radiator that made clanking noises all night long in winter. Each night I would pull my extra-long window shade all the way down, and then rest my giant alarm clock on the shade on top of the windowsill. This way, if someone tried to get in through the window the shade would fly up, causing the alarm clock to fall on the radiator making a smashing noise that would either scare off the intruder or wake me in time to run downstairs and out the door. It was like the game of Mouse Trap, each piece carefully and deliberately placed to set off a chain reaction. If the intruder chose to enter through my bedroom door, I also had piles of clothes, stuffed animals, and other noisy junk strewn about to alert me.

This was my well thought out plan. I began my catastrophizing early. This experience is also my excuse for my chronic messiness, which continues today. I feel more comfortable when things are a little all over the place. I don't totally trust an uncluttered space, which makes me a kind of a hypocrite when I pester my kids to clean up their rooms.

I was a latchkey kid growing up, so when my parents were at work or out or away on trips for both business and pleasure for what sometimes felt like forever, I was mostly home alone or with my older brother, Michael. We learned the rules of protecting ourselves on the streets of NYC quickly and they became second nature. We knew how to walk with a purpose. We knew that if we were followed coming home from school (as I was multiple times), we should go to the gas station across the street instead of to our front door to tell the people there what was happening. We knew not to make eye contact with strangers and stay in groups as much as possible.

When our parents were not home, Michael did most of the cooking and he was an amazing cook even as a teenager. We only had one grease fire in the kitchen, and again being somehow savvy about these things, Michael knew to throw a blanket over it rather than pouring water on the flames. Unfortunately, we used my mom's "good" blanket and when she and my dad returned home from wherever they'd been that night, they were pissed. But we were secretly proud of ourselves. We had survived and we thought it was worth a nice blanket. And when my bedroom booby trap didn't feel quite secure enough, I would sneak into my brother's room and sleep on the top bunk of his bunk bed while he slept below, never noticing I was there. Close to him, with the noise from the street, I felt safe.

These were the steps I had to take to feel physically safe as a child. And by the time I was a teenager, hitting a man with a hero was second nature. However, at this age, when it came to my emotions, I had learned it wasn't safe to express them. Too many feelings meant I would be told I was too needy, too difficult, and open myself up to rejection or shame. And so to protect myself emotionally I developed a system, a set of rules to live by, just as I had done before to protect my physical self. People pleasing was a big one. That's why I took that damn hero in the first place: to please my friend and not leave her with the remnants of all of this lunch meat as if nobody cared.

1. Please the people

And also:

2. Don't focus on your feelings
3. Agree with what others say and feel about you
4. Don't draw too much attention to yourself
5. Don't be too needy
6. Don't eat too much
7. Hide your weirdness
8. Control everything

This became my emotional playbook for moving through the world, which means I basically hid my true self. These rules didn't really work for me because I couldn't *always* please people or avoid needing. And sometimes I was hungry. Somewhere deep inside, I didn't agree with the thoughts and statements around me and in my head. Things felt out of control. But I kept trying to follow the plan. And every time I strayed, I didn't question the plan itself. I just figured that I was flawed.

When I became a parent, I thought I would be able to emotionally protect my kids in a way that I'd never felt protected. Then I could be an actual hero. Their hero. I made a conscious effort to help them be themselves and love themselves, whatever stages of self-discovery they went through. I was sure I was getting it right. I wanted them to feel emotionally safe. These were not children told to quiet their feelings; nobody heard "man up" and "stop crying." These were kids who were encouraged to show emotion and tell people how they felt, to say I love you when they felt love, to say NO with ease and YES with excitement. They were shown how to be careful with their own hearts and those of other people. They were shown how to apologize with meaning and learn and reflect. I worked hard at giving them all the examples I wished I had had. I was absolutely parenting myself while parenting them. I wanted them to know they were valued. We celebrated the weirdness, and they were allowed and encouraged to need and feel. I was going to be right there to save them from all of life's drama and trauma, and in doing all of that, I would heal my own little girl.

My playbook for them was:

1. Feel the feelings
2. Decide for yourself who you are
3. Need
4. Ask for what you need
5. Eat
6. Be weird
7. Let go

One afternoon we were all on the playground. The twins were around five, and Jesse must have been four. Jacob had been going through a period when he would only wear his soft and comfy striped pajamas. It wasn't a battle worth fighting so we just leaned in. That day, a kid we didn't know joined us on the jungle gym. He gave Jacob "the up-down" and asked, "Why are you wearing your pajamas? It's daytime." The mama bear in me wanted to get angry and yell at this poor little kid. How dare he ask what I had decided was such an obviously critical and judgmental question. The little girl in me was afraid. Afraid that Jacob might feel pain or shame like I had. I wanted to tell this kid to go away and stop being mean. Of course, he was only being a curious kid, and I was in my brain, totally overreacting.

I took a breath, and eager to protect my son, I quickly answered for him, without giving Jacob a chance to say anything himself. I asked the child, "Why did you wear that T-shirt today?" He responded by saying "Because I like it." And I said, "And that is why he is wearing his pajamas." The answer was satisfying for the kid and for me, and I assumed for Jacob as well, and the two of them went on to play. But later, Jacob came to me and asked why I had answered for him. He told me he could have done it himself. And in that moment, I realized that by constantly jumping in to rescue my kids at the first sign of distress, I wasn't allowing them to practice. I wasn't letting them figure out how to come to their own rescue.

Growing up, I often felt like I had to leap without a net, not knowing if anyone had my back. I resented having to figure so much out alone, so when I became a parent, I decided that what my kids needed from me was to jump in and run interference. But damn, I had it all wrong.

It would take me some time to realize that it wasn't my job to rescue my kids when they were struggling. I was teaching my kids to embrace who they are, to be needy, to ask, to feel and to love precisely so that *they* could come to their *own* rescue. What I wanted was for them to know that I would always be there in the background, rooting for them. I had their backs, but they could do it without me. Maybe Jacob's response on the playground would have gotten a different reaction than mine. Maybe he would have been hurt or maybe not. But as scary as this idea might have been—for *me*, not for *him*—I had to step back and give him—give each of my kids—the chance to be themselves, to save themselves. That is how I could be brave. That is how I could be a hero.

When I left Jacob's room that night after telling my "hero" story to his friends, I stood outside thinking about the group of beautiful, quirky, messy teens gathered in his room. I had known many of them for years and was privy to a lot of the drama and trauma they had already suffered or were in the midst of suffering. And for a moment, I worried about Jacob, and his friends, and Ben and Jesse too. I listened a while longer outside the door, hearing the murmurs of deep conversation followed by belly laughs, and I knew that somehow, they would make their own plans to get through. They had each other and the tools and the stories. And just like I had, just like we all do, they would figure it out. They would be OK.

I honor my strength and courage.
I am my own hero.

CHAPTER 8

KEEP ON LOVING

Two of my three kids are in love right now. Or at least they think they are in love. Maybe when they are older and in other relationships, they will look back and realize, like many of us do, that they may have only *thought* they were in love, and that real, adult love is something different. Or maybe they will look back and say they absolutely and definitively were in love. Depending on how their current relationships end and how new relationships feel, they will decide. But for now, we are all living in the moment, as if these are the great loves of their lives, the only relationships they will ever have.

What I like about watching my kids in their relationships is that, from what I can see, they are completely and totally themselves. With their current significant others, they are just as weird and expressive, and anxiety ridden, and quirky as they are in the safety of their own home. When Ben called from boarding school and told me about having a girlfriend, one of the first things I asked him was "Are you as wonderfully wacky with her as you are with us?" Thankfully his answer was "Yes, of course!" Since Jesse, unlike Ben, is living at home, their relationship is happening right in front of me and I get to witness their openness and vulnerability and see that they aren't changing who they are to make anyone else feel comfortable. I see the deep friendship they are cultivating with their partner. It is beautiful.

My kids know I love love. I am especially obsessed with movies about young love. They roll their eyes at me because they know I can't get enough of the drama and intensity of emotion, even when the story lines are sappy. They know one of my favorite rom-coms of all time is *Notting Hill*, and I am known to quote the (all too familiar) line "I'm just a girl, standing in front of a boy . . ." just to get on their nerves. They know I am always down to watch a cheesy high school romance like *The Kissing Booth* (don't judge). As predictable and "extra" as these movies are, I love them because I can live vicariously through characters and get caught up in the scripted drama. I can remember the intensity of young love and new love. I can experience the rush with a great soundtrack making it that much more intense and beautiful. I can pretend for just a couple of hours that love with its messiness and yet predictable twists and turns somehow always works out in the end and put aside what I know about the realities and complexities of love off the screen.

I was a senior in high school the first time *I* fell in love. I had a job after school and on weekends at a high-end clothing store on the Upper West Side in Manhattan. I was contemplating a career in fashion at that time and this job was a dream for me. It was retail, so naturally it wasn't all glamour. But it gave me access to sample sales and discounts on beautiful designer clothes, and despite all the folding and the high-maintenance customers it was worth it. It also made me feel like a grown-up and allowed me to find my people outside of school, which was a breath of fresh air. And of course, there was a paycheck. My coworkers were all a bit older and so chic and gorgeous. There was a men's store and a women's store right next door to each other. The stores no longer exist but I imagine that if they did, today they would have merged, understanding more about gender nonconformity and unisex clothing. But this was the late eighties, and that's how it was.

I fell hard for a guy named Scott, who worked in the men's store. He was nineteen and I was seventeen. I had lots of male friends at school, but he was the first one who gave me butterflies and I just wanted to be around him all the time. He was fun and cute and we both loved fashion. We laughed and were goofy and could share secrets and what we thought were "deep" emotions. Despite my feelings for him, our relationship never really got romantic, and I would find out later that he was gay. Looking back, I guess there were signs. He did have a group of equally fit and beautiful male friends who would meet him after work often and they would all go to the gym, but I thought nothing of it. He was just a beautiful boy who was kind and made me laugh and loved the same things I loved and cared about me.

I took Scott to my senior prom. The junior prom had been a disaster. I had invited a boy from another school who I also lost my virginity to. I was NOT in love with him. I remember asking my mother (after the fact) if you needed to be in love with someone to sleep with them. This was a rare instance of me confiding in my mother—typically, I would not have shared the details of my dating life with her. Her answer was "no," which made me feel slightly better since this guy had been an awful date and spent most of the night dancing with another girl in my class.

Senior prom was different. Scott was impeccably dressed, and I had designed and made my own gown, which I thought was gorgeous (though keep in mind, it was the eighties). We pulled out all the stops, each chipping in for a limo which took us to a very chic downtown New York restaurant called the Odeon. It was a bit over the top, but made us feel glamorous and grown-up.

After dinner, Scott and I got stoned in the limo and went to the prom, showing up appropriately late for extra mystery. I don't remember where it was, but I do remember that Scott was by my side all night. He danced with only me. He was amazing with my friends and knew just how to make my frenemies jealous. He even kissed me on the dance floor, which I can't imagine was fun for him, but he made me feel cool and cared for. Everyone wondered who he was and where I had found such a stunning boy.

Scott was also responsible for taking me to the nightclub that changed my life. After prom was over, he told me he had a surprise and directed the limo to take us to Nell's, which would soon become a place that felt like home to me and where I would meet my beautiful chosen family. With Scott by my side, we were whisked right in past the velvet ropes and into a place of pure joy. Other friends from work were there and we danced until closing time. It was a magical night. Ultimately, my heart would be broken, not because Scott had done anything wrong, but because we were obviously not meant to be. It was painful for me, but he was living his truth and I learned how to move past the ache of lost love, which is a rite of passage for everyone.

Since Scott, I have had other relationships that were fun and amazing and dramatic. I have loved men for their creativity, for their beauty, for their intelligence and excitement, for their sense of humor. However, with most of these relationships, I recognized and accepted that our time together was temporary. This did not mean that I wasn't all in, for however long it lasted. I savored every minute. But I wasn't *in* love with any of these men. Even with the kids' father, Evan, who I was in a relationship with and then a marriage for almost nineteen years, I was not in love. Though I wanted to be, and I thought I was for a time, I wasn't. To me, *in love* means partnership, communication, laughter, fun, seeing and accepting someone for everything that they are, weirdness and all, wanting to do the work when it is hard, and, of course, some butterflies along the way. With Evan, I felt the butterflies, and, in the beginning, I thought he saw me and seemed to embrace the weirdness but that quickly changed, and the rest never came. When we got together, he was coming out of a difficult marriage, and he wanted attention and support and excitement from our relationship. I was drawn to him because of that but also because he seemed gentle, stable, and grounded. He was also less sophisticated and worldly than I thought I was, which made me feel useful and powerful. I felt like I had something to offer because I could teach him the ways of the world, being a city girl and all. He was everything I believed I needed to balance out my wild and chaotic side and also to make me believe I was necessary. He was reliable and good-looking, and he irritated my parents just enough to make him even more appealing. The fact that he had been married before and already had children did not thrill them. In my mind, I thought his having kids would make him a great father to the children I hoped we would have together, since he would know how to be a parent. In retrospect, we were doomed from the beginning. It turned out each of us *needed* the other to fill a hole, an emptiness, something about ourselves and our lives we thought was missing. What I really needed was to work on loving myself, so I could bring a whole person to a relationship, or at least a more self-aware one.

Instead, we looked to each other to complete ourselves. Though we were dating for ten years and married for nine and would have three children together, we would never figure out a partnership that worked. It wasn't all terrible; some of it was amazing. We had vacations and dinners and laughter and moments of connection. But ultimately, it seemed Evan did not like my weird. To him, it was not wonderful. I felt that I was required to change myself, to hide myself in order to make him feel secure. And in all fairness, I was obviously not comfortable with myself as I was willing to try to go along with being someone else. And I didn't embrace all of who he was either. Everything between us became burdensome instead of loving or accepting. The deterioration of our marriage was slowly building like a wave until it crashed on the shore, and I found myself gasping for air.

In the beginning, it was easy to dismiss the red flags. I couldn't be bothered to notice that certain things were a problem. I could give up my male friends like he asked; I could stop going clubbing like he insisted. I could even tolerate the constant, baseless accusations of infidelity that came out of nowhere. I was busy, in school, teaching, throwing parties with my work friends. And then as soon as we married my focus became on having kids, which wasn't happening easily and was full of challenges. There were so many doctor's appointments and tests and finally a round of IVF (we were very lucky it took the first time), then twins and the surprise of a third very shortly after. My children then became my main focus, distracting me from the building contempt and the growing disconnect that was my marriage. As soon as they were born, it seemed to me that Evan pulled back, right away letting me know he would not be getting up in the nighttime to share duties as he worked as a builder with heavy machinery and needed his rest. He seemed annoyed about participating in ways that might relieve me of some of the parenting duties. He had made me promise, before the kids were born, that I would put him first. I did. But really how could I have meant that? The love I felt and feel for my kids was and is like nothing else and I knew they would always come first even in the best relationship. He seemed to resent this, and me. I resented him for refusing to be present, for not helping me more with the babies. I felt like I was doing it all alone. Our relationship became transactional. It went something like this:

Him: If you give up your free time (the moments to yourself when our children are sleeping or in preschool) and don't choose exercise, yoga, writing, or breathing over me, if you focus on my needs, and I know I am more important than you, I will help you with our children. If you "behave" and don't flirt or make eye contact with other men, even your coworkers, then I will give you my attention. If you aren't enough for me, then I will withdraw.

Me: If you help me with the children, if you let me exercise or choose time for myself, without guilt, I will give you my attention.

I found a strange familiarity in the discomfort of our relationship. I assumed that this was just my new normal and that we would remain this way forever. As much as I realize it's a cliché to have "daddy issues," it was similar to what I had experienced in my relationship with my father: My feeling of never being "enough," what felt to me like controlling behavior and the anger, quieter with Evan than with my father, but just as present and painful. My parents' relationship was loud and tumultuous. There was often yelling, and I saw them hurt each other over and over with their words and their actions. Yet they stayed together. Yet they had laughter and moments of kindness and were fiercely protective of each other. They were attached, codependent. I rarely witnessed them calmly sharing deep thoughts or working through issues together. But they must have figured something out, something that kept them together for fifty years. And as a kid, I didn't know the complexities of their relationship and I found its extreme highs and lows confusing. As I started having my own relationships, I knew I wanted something different, some consistency and calm. Maybe I set the bar too high. Maybe my expectations of love were ultimately unattainable. But I had seen other couples make it work. I had seen my friends' parents act with calm kindness toward each other. Of course, no one ever really knows what is happening behind the scenes.

For years, I was slowly drowning in my marriage. The disconnect and the loss of myself, the lack of partnership in caring for our children were heavy and lonely. In the rare moments, when I was by myself, without kids around, I would lie in the dark on the floor of my closet and cry, wondering if I would forever be stuck here in this relationship I knew was not working, was not love. Ultimately, the idea of being alone seemed like a better option than being lonely within my relationship. That kind of loneliness was too much to bear. What my children were witnessing between their parents wasn't loud and chaotic, but it wasn't loving either. Evan and I were passive-aggressive, quietly angry, and sad. We were completely disconnected. I knew I needed something to shift. We needed something to shift. The therapy didn't help. The attempts to fake the niceties as the therapist suggested until they became real never got us anywhere but further apart. Finally, I asked Evan to move out. I think he was furious with me because it hadn't been *his* choice. He seemed willing to stay in this unloving marriage forever even if he too wasn't happy or in love. He didn't want another divorce and thought we would just muddle through. But it couldn't go on. We had to break the news to the children who were nine and ten at the time. He refused to be a part of the conversation which felt like his way of punishing me. It was up to me. Once again, I had no parenting partner.

I remember walking with them down our long driveway toward the mailbox, trying to find the words, and finally saying "Your dad and I are not going to live together anymore. We are not finding happiness with each other, but our love for you will always be the same and he will not be far away." Or something to that effect. It's such a hard thing to explain. There is so much you want your kids to understand, but there are no words to capture it all. I didn't want them to feel responsible. I wanted them to know that sometimes a romantic relationship doesn't work out, but that love between parents and children is different and permanent. I wanted them to know that in their own lives, they had choices and options. There was so much that I wanted to express, far more than they could take in as young kids. What a strange thing for a child to navigate. The different kinds of love. Between couples, between parents and children. What lasts and what doesn't. And how do you know for sure? The idea that they might question the depth and permanence of their father's love and my love for them as a mom scared me most of all. When I told them what was happening, I was afraid for sure. I didn't know what they might say or feel. How could I? Instead of trying to anticipate it all I tried to let go of any expectations about what their responses might be, hoping they wouldn't fall apart but aware they might. As they have all their lives, each had a different reaction. Ben asked if his dad and I could try harder. Jesse told him we had already tried hard, and it obviously wasn't working (how they knew that I have no idea). Jacob asked to go lie down.

More questions came and I tried to answer the best way I could. Evan moved into a rental close by and we all did our best to make it all OK even if sometimes it wasn't. They got through it. We got through it. I know they carry the scars of a divorce within them, and I carry the thoughts that I somehow have failed by not showing them what a loving, lasting romantic relationship can look like. Perhaps somehow, I have failed because I am still trying to figure it out for myself. They never got to witness from their parents how two people can work together through the good and the bad. I wonder sometimes if they think less of me because of that. In the beginning of our uncoupling, Evan and I struggled as co-parents. For a while after the divorce, I continued to resent how much still fell on my shoulders and wondered, now that he was physically out of the house and had already been distant when he was living with us, what things would be like between him and the kids. It has taken time, but as they have gotten older, the kids have cultivated their own loving relationship with their father, and he shows up in the best way he knows how for me and for them and that is worth a lot. Although I wish I had been in love with Evan and we had given our children a different example, in the end, I have no regrets about the marriage because it got me to where I am today, with these three miraculous, beautiful children. I learned I had choices and the strength to make them and more clarity for the next time around. I do hold onto a tiny bit of worry that each of my kids will not know how to find a true partner who sees them and that maybe they will be complacent or lose themselves in their own relationships, because that is what they saw between me and their father. But I have more hope than worry because what I am seeing so far in these first relationships is the opposite of what I struggled with and perhaps the lesson they learned is what NOT to do and that is OK too.

My kids haven't seen me in a *long-term* loving relationship, but they did finally see me in love once, for a brief period, and then they witnessed the me with a broken heart. A few years ago, I reunited with someone I had known forever. He had been my babysitter's boyfriend when I was twelve years old. We met one summer when I was staying at our beach house under the supervision of this babysitter. My parents weren't around, which was typical, but I loved being there despite the babysitter situation. I had friends from the city who were also at the beach for the summer, and friends who lived there year-round. I was happy to be with all of them and not to be riding the subway in the city for those hot, sticky months. Amy, the sitter, was twenty-one and beautiful. She did not seem to relish being a babysitter but instead appeared to have taken the job for the perks of its location and the ability to flirt and tan and strut around in her bikini, which was super embarrassing to me with my awkward twelve-year-old body.

One day, when she came to pick me up from tennis lessons, there was a gorgeous local boy, Steven, working at the tennis club stringing racquets. Amy jumped right in and they started having a summer fling. She would disappear for hours at a time with Steven, leaving me home alone or dumping me off at a friend's house so she could go out with him. At eighteen, Steven seemed like a man to me, and at a certain point, for some reason, he started inviting me to tag along with them instead of leaving me behind. Maybe he felt sorry for me. Who knows. He was kind and fun, and he made me feel like he genuinely really cared about me. He was also so cool driving around in his black Jeep, and of course I developed a secret crush.

At the end of the summer, Amy was finally gone, and I assumed during the year, I would still get to see Steven on the weekends when my family and I would come back to the house. We ran into each other a few times, and when we did, we exchanged a quick, joyful hello and a hug that was everything to me. There was always a feeling of warmth and safety. But life went on and there was high school and college and eventually we lost touch.

When Evan and I met and decided to move in together, I became a year-round resident in this beach town. Over the years, I had heard occasional news of Steven, but I hadn't given him much thought. I knew he had gotten married and had two children, but not much else, and I was busy living my own life. It wasn't until I started teaching the nursery kids at the local elementary school and I got my class list that I saw—holy crap!—his daughter was one of my students! It had to be the universe bringing us together again. There was no hint of romantic anything; I was in a relationship and so was he. But those feelings of comfort and safety and happiness mixed in with a little flirtation returned, and now he would get to see me as a grown-up and not an awkward twelve-year-old. The hugs at pickup and drop-off were still filled with warmth and comfort. He made me feel like our time together when we were younger was special to him (in a nonsexual way) when he brought me some old photos he had kept of us at the beach or by the pool that summer we met. It was a blissful year for many reasons, as I loved being a teacher but also because of the connection he and I still felt with each other.

After his daughter moved on and ended up going to a different school, our relationship once again became the occasional running into each other and sharing a hug and a quick catch-up. Those hugs were powerful though: electric and loving. Time passed and I divorced, then he divorced. One random day he reached out to me. He invited me for coffee and that was that. All over again, it was electric and magical and familiar and comfortable. He knew me. He saw my weirdness and accepted all of me without question or judgment and he shared his own, we didn't hold back, and it was beautiful. Things moved quickly from there. He said *I love you* first and early, and when it felt right, he met my kids and they adored him and I already knew his and we liked each other too. He and I had our own busy lives but made time to see each other at every opportunity, texted constantly, traveled, laughed a lot, and talked of a future together. I handed over a giant piece of my heart, slightly damaged from a marriage that shouldn't have been, but I didn't hesitate. I did it willingly, I was all in.

And then came the sudden shock and the heartbreak. He had gone to his son's college graduation upstate and the whole family was together for the weekend: his sister, ex-wife, daughter, all of them. But I wasn't worried. When he drove off I was there at his request to say goodbye. Our parting was full of its usual intimacies and sentiments of love. But days later when he returned, I felt a coldness and a distance that was familiar from past relationships that had run their course but was unexpected with this one. I tried not to pay attention to it, assuming it was just something in my own head. A day or two after he came back we drove to the beach where we often sat and sipped coffee and shared secrets, laughter, and words of love. This drive felt heavy from the start. I knew that this time something was different. We parked and he slowly shared the details of a weekend with his kids and his ex. As he spoke, I knew what was coming. I knew this was the end. He told me some BS story about having the chance to try again with his ex-wife, and he wanted to do so for the sake of his kids. He cried what I came to know were false tears. He talked about how much he loved my children. None of it made sense to me. His kids were grown. He and his wife had been apart for some time. I was so thrown that I reacted with humor instead of despair. I told a joke about having bought too many sundresses in anticipation of a summer together. But I was crushed. I later came to find out that he had done this a few times before, met and gotten involved with women and their children, before going back to his ex-wife when it all got serious or scary. I felt a sickness in the pit of my stomach that I hadn't experienced since being a teenager. I felt embarrassed, stupid, and silly. Obviously I didn't know him as well as I'd thought, or at all. It made me wonder if we ever really know anyone. Why had he been so careless with me? Why hadn't I been more careful with myself? Should I have guarded my heart until I knew it was safe to give a piece away? Is it ever safe? It's always a risk. Is it worth it?

My kids had finally witnessed me in love, and then suddenly, I was in a dark place with no warning. I tried to hide it from them, but they wanted to know why I couldn't eat and why they would find me lying on our deck, teary-eyed, for hours at a time. Why weren't they seeing Steven lately? I didn't want to explain what was going on. I changed the subject and made excuses. I wanted to keep them from seeing my heartbreak. Why should they have to learn that this happens, even to grown-ups? Why should they have to see me in another failed relationship? Would they be disappointed in me? Maybe they would think less of me or wonder if it's worth putting yourself out there. UGH. Wasn't I way too old to be going through this drama? Now my kids had to see it all. Eventually, my brother convinced me to tell them what was happening and what had happened. He pointed out that I was overthinking, as is my MO. He assured me that they would say something wise or supportive to help get me through. I was afraid but I took his advice. I tried very hard to calmly explain to my kids that Steven and I weren't going to see each other anymore and that he had the chance to be back with his ex-wife and with his kids. It was a reason that made him seem like maybe he was a decent guy. I think I didn't want them knowing I had been such a bad judge of character. I kept the details to myself, and I tried not to show them how angry and betrayed I felt, but I couldn't hide my sadness and my grief.

My brother had been right about sharing what I was going through with my kids. There was absolutely no judgment from them. Instead, they told me that they loved me. Even though I tried to make Steven seem like he wasn't a jerk, they saw through it all. Jacob commented on what a "dick move" this was, a phrase I didn't know he knew but fully appreciated. Ben told me that I was amazing and not to worry because I would find somebody who deserved me. They each told me they had been glad to see me happy and that I would be again. It was as if they had been through this before. They knew just what to say. Their words filled my soul and their love helped me heal. I lost the love of a partner, but I felt the love between myself and my kids. The unconditional love that allowed me to be vulnerable without judgment but only support and comfort. That love reminded me to go easy on myself and not to blame or shame myself but keep on loving me. After time had passed and with lots of hugs I was able to reflect on the experience. Although the reflection and the retelling come with a little ache they also come with a little gratitude for what I did have, even for a short time, and what I learned for the next time, as I vow not to close myself off to what might be ahead.

I think back on that experience quite a bit now, as I watch my kids navigate their first loves. I see them being completely themselves without hesitation. Not changing for anyone, not asking anyone to change. Open and all in. I am fascinated by the way that they don't hide who they are or hold back. The way they already seem to know that a relationship isn't meant to replace what is missing or squash who you are. They are fearless. They make me want to be like they are. I wonder what can I possibly teach them about romantic love, as someone who hasn't figured it out yet? Perhaps they have learned from my mistakes, or maybe they love and trust themselves enough to know more than I did.

Maybe I need to stop trying to teach them, stop trying to protect them from heartbreak because in the end I can't. They will go through it and they will get through it and if they need me, I will be here for them as they were for me. Reminding them they will be able to share their hearts again. Maybe the best I can do is love them unconditionally and love myself; not hardened, not bitter, not afraid, but willing, open, unafraid, fearless, and still loving love. Maybe that is enough.

I choose to move through the world with an open heart.

CHAPTER 9

EXHALE

At some point in my yoga journey, I had a teacher who spoke about the concept of attachment and how to practice letting go. She said something like *before every inhale is an exhale*. It took me a minute to understand what she meant, and I am certain she ended the statement with a dramatic pause so that everyone in class could let her words sink in. Perhaps you already get it. It was such a simple way of explaining that to make space for something new (inhale), you have to first let something go (exhale). When you exhale you are letting go of that beautiful, life-sustaining breath you just took in. You can't hold onto it or get attached. It has to leave your body. But you can get curious and notice its quality, its depth. You can feel it nourish you, filling your chest, your belly, your back. Maybe it's fast and shallow or slow and deep. You can take in the information it gives you so that maybe the next breath can be slower or deeper if you need it to be. You can notice the pause between breaths, and when you have exhaled completely, it can be a moment of peace and gratitude, knowing you have made space for something amazing to enter.

I was recently speaking with a group of soon to be graduates of a children's yoga and mindfulness teacher training. Someone asked me what advice I would give to these new teachers, who were about to begin their journey of teaching yoga to kids. I am not one for shoulds, but in this case, I had some advice to offer. I told the group that teaching yoga to kids is not about bringing all the props or games, and it's not about lesson plans and poses and specific meditations. In fact, it has almost nothing to do with what you teach your yoga students. It's about YOU, teachers. My advice? Let go.

My earliest experiences of teaching kids' yoga were awful. The very first class I taught was probably one of the worst. I had completed multiple levels of yoga teacher training and coupled with my elementary school teaching degrees and my time as a kindergarten teacher, I felt more than prepared. I had learned how to take all ages of kids through sequences of poses. I'd studied how to support kids who had suffered trauma and how to make my yoga classes inclusive. I had learned when to keep things secular and when to throw in some namastes and oms. I had extensive knowledge of the physical, mental, and the quantifiable academic benefits of yoga in schools—better focus, improvement of test scores, less time spent on classroom management. I also had my own practice, and I was a mom.

So, in my ego brain, I felt I was obviously *over*qualified to teach my first class. I was hired to teach at my own kids' elementary school, which was very progressive, and they wanted to add a yoga program to their curriculum. On this first day, I set up my room with props, mats, and glitter jars. I had music and shaky eggs and feathers. I had imagined that this would be every kid's favorite class and that I would take everyone through a beautiful sequence of poses and meditations and help them all breathe and feel relaxed and cultivate agency and control over their bodies and emotions. It would all be perfect, and this perfection was ensured by the fact that I had meticulously crafted and memorized a lesson plan.

The kids came into the room, oohing and aahing at all the fun props I had spent so much time setting up, seating themselves in a lovely circle. I started with some deep-breathing exercises, which went over well. Then we moved on to a name game using a bell. Each child was to take the bell, say their name, and then as slowly as possible, walk the bell to another student, the challenge being that they would walk so quietly and mindfully that the bell wouldn't ring. It went to hell in less than ten seconds.

The first child picked up the bell, yelled his name "Lukas!" and proceeded to run around the circle ringing the bell as loudly as he could. As soon as this happened, all the other kids jumped up and began to chase him, and suddenly the whole group was running in circles, and everything was chaos. I think I sat speechless for a few moments while the kids were circling the room in what felt like a *Lord of the Flies* situation. I spent the rest of our time together just trying to rein them all in without yelling or bursting into tears.

When it was over and I was alone, my first thought was that I wasn't cut out for this after all. There would be no lives changed here. Not with me at the helm. What had I been thinking? I couldn't even get these kids to follow a simple lesson plan. Before I got too deep, I considered telling the school that they had made a mistake and that I was resigning. But of course, I didn't do that. I went home, had a good cry, and then I took a shower and a long pause and reflected on the experience. What had really gone wrong?

I realized that I had been so focused on the outcome, on this vision I had for how everything should go, that I set myself up for disaster and disappointment. I hadn't left room for any other experience. I hadn't stayed open to the unexpected or whatever might present itself and require me to adapt and shift. I had forgotten that all kids (all humans) have different energy levels, different attention spans, and different interests and that I needed to be able to roll with that.

I like control and I like a plan. I like to be able to consider all possible outcomes. I also know that if I want to teach yoga to children, I need to be willing to surrender these attachments. I need to let them go. This was the reason I wanted to teach yoga to kids in the first place, so that they too could learn not to focus on outcomes or to hold on too tightly to their emotions and thoughts. Rather than being overwhelmed by their big feelings, I wanted to teach them to notice these feelings, to get curious about them, and to know that they will pass. But before I could teach these things,

I had to be willing to do them myself. And so that evening, after my terrible first day as a yoga teacher, I decided to let go, as hard as it was, because holding on was always my first instinct. I made a commitment to myself to return to class the next day, and the day after that, and practice staying open to what might happen. There would be chaos *and* calm. There would be kids who were into it and those who were not. There would be good days and bad. And I knew somewhere in me, I had the ability and tools to go with the flow instead of trying to force a result.

My brother Michael and I have a little thing we say to each other, whenever we're celebrating a win or achievement in our lives. After giving each other the proper and heartfelt amount of "Yays" and "Amazings," we follow up with "Don't get too attached." We say it with sarcasm, because this is what we learned as kids, not to get too attached to anything good. Because we are flawed and there is always some impending doom or disappointment on the horizon that is sure to arrive and crush our joy. "Don't get too attached." We say it, and then we laugh with an edge of anger and sadness. We both recognize the absurdity of the messaging we got as kids: We were expected to attain perfection, but because we were inherently worthless, we would never get there. We would never be enough. Our flash of achievement would be just that, a flash, followed quickly by failure to remind us of our flaws. Even little things like sharing a good grade with my father led to these reminders. I would say, "Look, Dad! I got a ninety-eight!" His immediate response, in all seriousness, would be "What happened to the other two points?" Don't get too attached to that good grade. Don't get too attached to the idea that you'll succeed. Don't get too attached to feeling good about yourself.

Despite the origins of this phrase for both of us, ultimately, Michael and I are right to practice not getting too attached. Not because we are bound to fail and are not worthy, but because by accepting that nothing is permanent, we can appreciate and celebrate the good as it comes. And we can let go of the losses rather than lingering on them. We appreciate that the next experience is just around the corner, and soon our circumstances, our mindsets, our emotions will shift.

My three children have been the ultimate test of my ability to let go. As a mama, I have learned that it is completely futile to focus on outcomes, no matter how much I might want something to happen. Similar to that first day of teaching yoga, there is a story involving my kids as toddlers that always reminds me of this. When they were three and four, I used to take the kids to a special beach near our house. There were rarely other people on this beach, the sand was covered with fun shells to collect, and the water was filled with little sea creatures to watch. It was a magical place where I could let the kids roam free without feeling like I had to keep an eye on their every move. Usually, it was just the four of us there, but one afternoon, when Evan was off from work, we decided to have a family beach day.

In my mind, this beach trip was going to be perfect. We would be together as a family, having fun and playing, and Evan would see what the kids and I did without him, and he would want to join us more. I had so much riding on this outing. We loaded up the car with beach gear and snacks and put on sunscreen, and we were off. About eight minutes from the beach Jesse started feeling carsick and proceeded to projectile vomit everywhere. It was a mess, Jesse was crying, and we could have turned around, but we were determined to get to the beach and make this day happen. We decided the solution was to rinse Jesse in the water when we arrived. When we finally got there, we did this, and for a while, all was well. We were still having our family beach day.

Then, after we'd been at the beach for maybe twenty minutes, almost simultaneously, Ben was stung by a jellyfish and Jacob stepped on a razor clam. As Ben began to scream, Jacob began to bleed and the blood wouldn't stop, and neither would the screaming. We grabbed everyone and everything, got back in the car, and headed straight for the pediatrician, where Ben was consoled by the doctor and Jacob received his first set of stitches (there would be many more).

There went the plan. There went our perfect afternoon. When we all got home, sandy and exhausted, I realized that this was probably going to be the way it was forever with kids. Not the injuries and vomiting (although there was plenty of both), but the plans and the outcomes that were never exactly what I had expected or hoped for. The strange turn of events. And there was nothing I could do to change this. I could have wallowed in self-pity and agonized over what might have gone differently if only I'd realized that Jesse would get carsick or if only I'd paid more attention to the other two in the water. But none of that would have done any good. The next thing was around the corner, and if I was going to have any shot at doing this parenting thing well, I would need to get over myself. I would need to be able to surrender, pivot, and adjust in the moment. I had no choice. I had to learn to let go. To exhale. To make space for the next inhale. Or at least to try.

Today, with my kids, I am on the verge of what feels like the ultimate loss of control: having an empty nest. I have two rising seniors and one junior who will be moving on sooner than I can handle. Emotionally, my kids are already there, living their private, mysterious, and dramatic teenage lives from which I am mostly excluded. Intellectually, I know this is meant to be and it's so much better that they are separating and individuating rather than still clinging to me and relying on me for everything. But in my emotional brain, it feels like the brakes on my car are busted and I am approaching the top of a hill and about to go flying down the other side with no way of stopping.

I find myself trying to pump the brakes by telling them to pick up their clothes, clean their rooms, take a shower. I nag them to check their emails and call their grandma. I was recently on a college visit in San Francisco with Jacob, and just before we boarded our flight home, I asked him whether he had brushed his teeth that morning. His response was no, because we had left our hotel for the airport at four A.M. For some reason, this set me off and I began lecturing him about his teeth and caring for himself and life choices. By the time we boarded the plane, we were both frustrated with each other. As he slept for the next six hours, I stayed awake and I began asking myself why I had picked the fight. Why had I bothered him about brushing his teeth, something that at eighteen he of course knew how to do all on his own? I realized that I was still trying to hold on, to have control over something no matter how small. I could not seem to let go.

After the flight I apologized to Jacob, and without squashing his excitement I tried to express to him that my behavior was a reflection of the sadness I was feeling about him leaving for college. I called Ben and Jesse and also shared my feelings, explaining the reasons behind my current micromanaging of their lives. Now, when I ache in my heart and feel sick in my stomach at the thought of my children moving on, I still feel it, but I also try to let it pass and to open myself up to the moment we are in. It is a practice, but I know if I can surrender to their growth and expansion and unstoppable entrée into adulthood, I will be able to let go and make space in my life and in theirs for whatever experience comes next and for the excitement that awaits.

Exhale . . .

Surrender . . .

Let go . . .

Make space . . .

Inhale . . .

This is the conversation I continue to have with myself. This is my practice. Make your plan. It can give you an intention, some structure and a feeling of safety. Then prepare to toss it aside and be present to what actually happens. There will be mess and chaos. There will be unexpected feelings. There will be success and failure. And once in a while it all goes just as you wanted it to. Sometimes it's even better. Let yourself celebrate the small wins and the big ones. Give your disappointment, sadness, anger a little loving attention and ask them why they have shown up, what do they need to tell you? Expand and contract with the moment. Then let it all go. Nothing will ever be perfect or permanent. A new experience is around the corner. Exhale. Don't get too attached.

With every deep breath,
I let go and make space for
something beautiful.

CHAPTER 10

IN THE STILLNESS

am in the driver's seat of my car sitting next to my father, who is in the passenger seat. It's late October and I have just picked him up. His home is a short walk from the beach but my father can no longer take this walk. He is barely able to manage the few steps from his door to the car without leaning on me like a wounded hiker. After the two-minute drive, we are in the beach parking lot facing the ocean. This has been our daily ritual for the last couple of weeks as he has become less able to leave the house or even really hold up his own body for any significant length of time.

As soon as we found out he had pancreatic cancer, I knew it was a death sentence. This is a cancer for which there is no cure. It was nearly impossible to wrap my head around it all as my father was always so healthy and busy and bragging about living to be at least one hundred years old like his own father. For my father, showing anything that resembled weakness was out of the question. Revealing, or rather admitting, that he had pancreatic cancer was probably the most difficult thing he had to do in his life. He got his diagnosis two weeks before he shared it with anyone. Later we would realize that during those initial two weeks, he had gone into overdrive, his usual "action" mode times ten. Alone, he had found himself an oncologist and then he immediately began researching all the clinics overseas that were working on pancreatic cancer and making claims about successfully treating or eradicating it. He began contacting them and making plans to travel. He did coffee enemas and drank protein shakes and tried any other "cure" he read about on the Internet. Until finally he took a breath and realized he would have to share the news with his family. He was already in pain by the time of his diagnosis and he had lost a lot of weight. His doctor told him he needed a port put in his body for his take-home chemo treatment. There was no hiding it anymore.

He sat the family down and told us in a very matter-of-fact way. Rather than panicking, I went into a kind of "mama bear" mode. I knew this was making him afraid and most definitely angry and suddenly I felt this instinctive need to be the one to take away his fear and comfort him. There was a cold calm that came over me, similar to the reaction I've had with my own kids when there were broken bones and split lips and trips to the emergency room. My mother, on the other hand, froze. The shock and terror made her literally immobile throughout the first few months of my dad's illness. She could barely get out of bed and seemed to move in slow motion. It was too much to go with him to his chemotherapy appointments. She couldn't bear to sit with him and watch him suffer and deteriorate. This wasn't about denial, it was just her reaction, and it took some time for her to get back to functioning.

Once we heard the words "pancreatic cancer," my mother, brother, and I weren't given the space or opportunity to dwell on our feelings. That was not what my father wanted. We were instead required to follow his lead and take ACTION. With my cold level-headedness, I was to be the one who would set the wheels in motion for all he was insisting we do. We were to figure out how to cure this incurable cancer. We had to get him started on the chemo and do all of the necessary Western medical treatments. We also had to look for alternative treatments, enter all the experimental trials, find him a therapist (up until now he had never believed in therapy for himself), and get the acupuncturist, yoga teacher, and nutritionist on board. Action is how we have always felt valued and important to my father. Action is how he has always valued himself. Move, achieve, DO. Don't waste time weighing options, just GO. And so, we did. But of course, none of that stopped the progression of this illness. Action didn't stop the brain fog and fatigue. It didn't stop the tumors in his liver from growing. It didn't stop the embolisms and the stroke that ended his ability to work and write, making it hard for him to walk and string thoughts together. But we all kept on acting.

In the midst of it all—the daily activities and phone calls and treatments and the deterioration of his health—while others were *doing*, I found myself focused more on *being*. Being softer with him, reading to him when he was no longer able, being by his side on his couch or outside looking at the beautiful trees in his yard. I wanted to take his hand, and I could see the scared little child that was very clearly present inside of him. It was this child I always thought about when I prepared to pick my dad up at his house for our drives to the beach. I carefully adjusted his seat like I had done so many times for my own kids when they were little (except they, of course, would be sitting in the back). I made sure that his heavy head would be supported and held in place and that there was a cushion for his protruding bones to lessen the pressure between his rail-thin body and the leather seat and a comfy blanket in case he was cold.

As the disease progressed, at times, he was unable to sit upright. Mostly he would either be lying down or seated at the kitchen table with his forehead resting on his crossed arms for support. Whenever I saw him like that, I thought about the number of times I had taught this "pose" to kids in their classrooms as a way to get some rest and relaxation without taking a full-on savasana. The pressure on their foreheads and the ability to just be in silence calms and quiets their minds and bodies. Kids loved it and I wondered if it was doing the same for him.

I took a bit of comfort in thinking this might feel good to him even though I was certain if he had the choice, he'd be his usual upright, energetic, blustery self. Most likely, off somewhere getting in a workout and drinking a smoothie before going into work or making a TV appearance somewhere. Because he was a prominent figure on Wall Street, he was a regular guest on some of the early morning finance programs like *Squawk Box* or Bloomberg TV. And I would be watching as per his request to make sure he was having a good hair day and so we could discuss the drama or points of view of the hosts. He'd be calling me to compare our daily exercise routines and compare weights and reps. He would definitely be wolfing down something more nourishing than the plain vanilla ice cream that is his meal du jour these days. Each time he makes it to the table, my mother or the many of us who were with him each day, anxiously serve him the ice cream in the same way. Two small scoops placed in a precious yellow bowl with a scalloped edge and a beautiful dessert spoon with a wooden handle resting in the bowl as the untouched ice cream slowly melts. I think this ritual gave my mom some hope that it might be enough to get him to eat and the feeling that she was doing something useful. This was the only food he showed any interest in when asked, and when it was placed in front of him, we all hovered around coaxing him like a child to take a few mouthfuls.

Eventually, the scoops became a soupy pool like the ones my brother and I would intentionally make as kids by furiously stirring the ice cream until we could joyfully slurp it directly from the bowl. There is no joy for him in these moments. It's hard to tell what he was thinking but he was not happy; he just looked exhausted. I was sure he heard the nervous whispers and was attuned to the anxious vibes surrounding him. Normally he would be telling us all to leave him alone or make some sarcastic remark about how none of us are actually helping, but for now he only had the strength to sit in a chair and lean his head on the table.

For all my life my relationship with this man had been busy and loud and intense. The times I felt he might possibly love me and not think of me as worthless or a disappointment were when we were in action. The spaces in between the moving were filled with yelling and criticism and fear, with a little bit of kindness and compassion thrown in just to keep us on our toes. Homework was always a trigger for him. We had this sort of routine where he would come to my room to "help" me and when I wasn't grasping concepts quickly enough or getting the answers right or I was asking too many questions, the yelling would begin, the insults would be hurled, and he would tell me I was going to fail as he stormed out of my room slamming the door in spite of the tears rolling down my face. An hour or so later he would return, calm and kind, and we would try again, usually with success. I knew this routine and I didn't interrupt it; I think I was hoping for an apology or a retraction, but that never came. Perhaps he thought just returning and speaking softly *was* the apology.

I later came to understand that my trauma began with his trauma. Growing up in a Jewish, working-class family in Oklahoma, the son of an alcoholic mother and a father who was mostly away serving in the navy, had shaped his experiences. He'd had no time or space as a kid for fear or resentment or reflection. He had been responsible for getting his mom home from the bar and helping her out at home, while studying, working, and making a life for himself. His inner voice was constantly catastrophizing, telling him stories of everything that could go wrong, which made him fearful and then angry. When he showed anger toward us, his family, he was acting out of fear for us and for himself. Taking action was what relieved that fear, making him feel worthy and in control. There was a point during his illness when he seemed to go into a kind of remission. He felt good, great actually. So great that he was told by his doctor he could travel, and we all longed for a big family vacation full of memories, but instead he chose to return to his office, to working, to his TV appearances. Although I wished he had chosen us, I understood. It wasn't vanity; it was just that work was what made him feel alive and capable and therefore unafraid.

Like most kids, I didn't see my parents as humans while I was growing up. I didn't see them as having a past and their own issues and, as a result, projecting their own stuff onto me. There was no separation between what they said and showed and how I thought they viewed me. There was no understanding that these might be their issues, not mine, until much later when I did the work for myself. This fear my dad had inside of him was managed with achievements, working, exercise, calorie counting, tennis games, going somewhere and doing something. Those busy moments were the ones in which I felt his approval and so I too kept moving.

Once I was older and living away from home, I began to accomplish things in my life that were visible and tangible—teaching, writing, becoming a mom. Because of those accomplishments, he yelled less, and we connected more. He could see the results of my actions and that calmed him. It made it easier for us to have a relationship. We spoke almost every day, chatting about our exercise routines, the manuscripts we were writing, his work, and things happening with my kids. He was elated every time I sold a new book or received an award or praise. These things meant he didn't have to be so afraid for me and the anger lessened.

I began to figure it out, the nature of our relationship. To feel loved by him I shared the glory and the list of things I was achieving. To love myself, I kept the struggles, emotions, and the inner work away from him, finding the tools to recognize my own worth: the yoga and meditation, the therapy and exercises in self-acceptance and contending with the battles in my head. I kept this for me alone. As my feelings about myself changed, my feelings about my relationship with my father also changed. The work I was doing for me trick-led down into how I showed up with him. I stopped resenting him so much and started feeling more compassion. I didn't feel the need to fight all the time and was learning how to create boundaries and untangle myself from his hurtful words, which were projections of his own self-worth.

About a year prior to his diagnosis, we had one last confronta-tion. It was BIG. Not for the yelling or intensity, of which there was a lot, but it was big because I took it as an opportunity to say everything that I had been keeping inside. My ex and I had just separated and sold our marital home, and I was living in a tiny house with my three kids. I was officially a single mom. It was daunting and stressful, and on top of it all Jacob's OCD was just starting to kick into full force.

My dad was an amazing grandpa and was over often to see the kids. It was clear to all of us how much he loved them. But on this day, something in him was triggered by Jacob's behavior. Maybe it reminded him of me when I was going through similar struggles as a kid that scared him or made him feel like something was happening beyond his control. Whatever the reason, I saw him transform into the father I had known from my childhood. The yelling began, and I can't even remember his words as much as his tone. Jacob cowered in the corner and then promptly ran to his room in tears. I could see the regret and the fear that instantly welled up in in my father. That was it though. I had been working so hard to make sure my children never had to feel unworthy the way I had. There was no way in HELL he was going to act that way with my kids.

I sent Ben and Jesse to check on their brother and play in another room, and then I said it all. All that I had felt as a child, all that I saw within him and understood about him, and all that I would NEVER allow in my home with my kids. I was a big girl. I was able to speak up and make clear that he would not see his grandchildren if this was in their future. I didn't want an apology or even reconciliation. I already knew I was good without that. It was in that moment that I had a chance to break the cycle, with compassion. After I spoke my piece, I didn't wait for a response. I just asked him to leave, and he did. I felt spent but also like there was nothing more to say. He now knew it all.

A few hours later, he called. He had heard me. Then there was an apology, what I had craved my whole life, but I didn't care anymore. I no longer needed the words; I only needed him to get it and to be different for my kids. He said he loved me and us. He promised he would take action, and that this time the action would be to do better. *That* was what I wanted to hear. I gave him a chance, knowing I had set the boundary and drawn the line. And he did it. He did better.

At first, when he got sick, I slipped back into the role of good girl and obedient daughter, following my father's instructions and jumping into action along with everyone else. My father wasn't yet open to emotional connection. Action is what he wanted from all of us and what he thought he needed. But as things progressed, action was no longer serving him. I saw this, and I began sneaking my practices into our time together. I started sharing some of my meditations, wondering at first if the stillness would bother him, if he would get too much into his head and feel like he wasn't doing enough. But after a while he seemed to crave these moments. He began to ask for more and started expressing more presence and contemplation. I wore a mala, a beautiful string of beads used for meditation (one bead, one breath), that was given to me by one of my best friends and he asked for one of his own, which he wore around his wrist just as I did mine. We would sit in the living room for hours, sharing only a few words about the nature of fire or dissecting the meaning behind the lyrics to the same songs he would play over and over.

Together, we started looking at the world in a way we never had before. There was a time when he wouldn't have had the patience for this kind of exploration and curiosity. He would have felt it was a waste of time. I began to notice that he longed to be in the present moment, to speak philosophically and to wonder about his relationship to the world. The need for action was fading. The action *around* him didn't stop but the action *within* him began to slow, and I became less afraid to be myself with him.

I had seen an opening, a way to find true connection between us. Not through sharing my accomplishments or showing him that I too could *do*. The reality was I could not do anything to stop him from dying. I could only hold space and hope that this was enough. I once did a training to learn how to use different modalities to help ease the discomfort of those who were dying. I learned specific body scan meditations and which essential oils were best for anxiety, pain, and nausea. I learned gentle movements for keeping the blood flowing and the brain active. In the training, as students we all practiced on one another. Because we were all healthy, we could only imagine what the practices would feel like for someone who was dying. Still, these practices for rest and self-care felt like heaven to us in the midst of our busy lives. But in real time, with someone, my father, who was actively dying, reaching for all of these tools and once again trying to *do* or *act* wasn't what he needed to be at ease. I learned that the most comforting thing I could do was not do and just be. To witness without projection or agenda and hold space for fear, for discomfort, for dying that allowed for dignity and a sense of peace.

So now, here we are, me and my dad facing the water for what will be our last time. Just the two of us in the parking lot ignoring the fifteen-minute parking sign, which nobody pays attention to in the fall anyway. The tourists have all gone back to NYC and it's just us locals (a concept I never have wrapped my head around as I still think of myself as a "city girl"). I've turned off the engine with no intention of leaving before we are ready. The East End of Long Island has some of the most beautiful beaches in the world. The sand is a soft beige, and the water is an ombre pattern of blues and greens. The waves are so big this time of year. Perfect for the surfers we can see from the car, as little dots rising and falling way offshore. Those dots show us how the ocean is breathing.

We have been to this beach so many times since I was a kid. I remember learning to dive into the waves with my dad. Holding his hand and just before we went under, I would feel like we might be crushed by the water smashing above us. But he would say take a deep breath and then pull me down before that thought had time to send me running back to shore. Maybe he didn't realize it, but water was always my father's calm, his meditation. He was obsessed with fishing and at one point bought a house in Argentina on a giant river. He would spend hours, days, weeks in that river alone casting over and over, not even caring about the catch. And he was never more present. He could describe the way the sun hit the water, the arc of the line. He could tell you the colors of the fish swimming just below the surface and the number of boulders and trees lining the river's edge. He was not thinking ahead or planning his next move. He was just being. Jacob seems to have inherited that connection with water. On land, his brain sends him into spirals of superstitious thinking. But he is a surfer and when he is on the water waiting for the next wave he is fully there, out of his head and in the moment. That is his meditation.

There we were in my car, sitting in silence, breathing with the waves, being. To me this was the most meaningful time my father and I ever had together. Even though I was hurting inside because I wanted more time, this kind of time, together. I wanted him to see my children grow and notice the ways in which they are like him and me and how they are also themselves. But here, in this moment, I could put that aside. There was no action, no competition, no projection. I didn't need to tell him all the ways he hurt me or show him all the things I have done well. In this stillness, there was no effort. I could feel that there was love.

When it was time, my brother and I stayed with him in the little room in his home with the hospice bed and the morphine drip, until he passed. We took turns through the night holding his hand and letting him know everything would be OK, even if we didn't know it ourselves. He died with the mala on his arm, which now sits on my own altar and brings me back to him.

That October morning at the beach was the last time we spent alone together. Father and daughter. Man and woman. Little boy and little girl. As I think about it all now, we could have done that moment differently. We could have tried to act and do and attempt to find the words to forgive and apologize and explain and wrap up a life lived together with a neat bow. But instead, we chose to be, to exist in that moment as if it defined our whole shared experience.

When I think about him now, I hear his voice in my head, sometimes hurtful and sometimes thoughtful, sometimes sharing a dad joke or two. In my mind I can see the two of us sitting next to each other, breathing with the ocean, watching the rise and fall of the surfer dots setting the pace. I am placing my hand on my heart, silently sending him loving kindness, wishing him peace and freedom from fear for whatever comes next. I see him frail but at ease, copying me like a child, putting his own hand on his heart and breathing along with me. Together we sit facing the water. Holding space, being. I know that I am enough, and so is he.

I am learning to sit in
stillness and without
judgment but with curiosity;
I notice what arrives.

CHAPTER 11

THE GIRL ON THE STOOP

Before I began compiling an inner dictionary of not enough-ness, before the critical voices strung the words together to define me, there was a little girl full of life and magic and feelings formed by the city that surrounded her. Although I've tried to push her away, to leave her behind, to blame her for my feelings about my own self-worth, this girl has always been inside of me. She appears in glimpses, asking to be heard and loved. She is the girl who comes out to dance with abandon in the kitchen with my kids. She is the one, full of wonder, who helps me see the world through my kids' eyes. She is the one who appears when I am living as my most authentic self. She is my intuition, my true north, and the one who takes my hand when I get lost in my fears and worries. She is the best parts of me. My little city girl.

This little girl is me, sitting on the stoop of my family's West Village brownstone. Ours was one of multiple brownstones lined up side by side, wrapping all the way around a square city block. We lived on the top two floors, and another family with kids lived on the bottom two floors. We took turns watching Sunday morning cartoons in each other's apartments; sometimes they came upstairs to us, sometimes we went downstairs to them. Eventually, the family with kids moved out, and a German sex therapist moved in who would complain to my parents about their "noisy kids" overhead while her patients waited for their appointments in the shared hallway. That complaint never prompted any "shushing" from my parents and definitely didn't stop us from being noisy. In fact, it probably made us noisier on purpose.

At a certain point, the symmetry of our square block of build-ings was interrupted by a big church that opened into a garden and courtyard that I could see clearly from my bedroom window. There were a lot of weddings in that church and the receptions were held in the garden courtyard. Sometimes my downstairs neighbor (one of the kids, not the sex therapist) and I would sneak into the early evening receptions, like Eloise crashing black-tie parties in the Plaza, except these weddings were much less fancy. It was the late seventies and everything was very relaxed and flowy. My usual outfit, when not crashing a wedding, was bell-bottom jeans, a white tee, and my Mork and Mindy rainbow suspenders. For weddings, I would spice things up a bit with a flowered skirt and knee socks. Oddly, whenever we got caught (which we always did), we were never reprimanded. Everyone seemed to think it was adorable that the neighborhood kids had snuck into their wedding, and they just sent us off with a laugh and usually a piece of cake.

From a young age, my brother and I were used to coming home to an empty apartment and feeding ourselves until my parents returned from work, travel, socializing, or some mysterious journey about which we didn't know the details. We didn't mind so much; we learned to navigate the city and embrace our independence from a young age. Across the street from our brownstone was a gas station managed by a nice man named Bubba, who came to my rescue a few years later, when I got off the bus coming home from school and was followed by a strange man. The rules of walking alone in the city had been drilled into me by my parents, so instead of going home and unlocking the front door with a potential mugger behind me, I knew to go to the gas station instead and tell Bubba what was happening. He had me stay by his side until the stranger was gone and then walked me across the street to make sure I made it safely inside.

There was a store just next to the gas station called the Pleasure Chest and because of its window display with mannequins in leather jockstraps mixed with policeman-style hats and handcuffs casually draped over their arms, for many years I thought it was a special store where policemen bought their underwear. A jazz club was on another corner and music was always playing and people stood in line to get in or just hung out in front to listen. Within walking distance, there were vintage shops and patisseries and pizza places, and everywhere there were people, always lots of people out in the streets moving about and making beautiful noise. They yelled, they laughed, and they lived and loved openly. And I was part of it—my voice added to the sounds, my presence added to the rhythm, and I felt necessary. It all filled me up, my block, my neighborhood, my city.

When we weren't sitting on our stoop or playing on our block, my brother Michael and I went to Washington Square Park to play on the swings or skateboard or people watch. Later, once I was a teenager, this park was the spot where my friends and I would meet up and hang out until it was late enough to make our appearance at the club. You didn't want to be too early. And it was our spot as little ones, too. At nine years old, Michael, a constant performer, was putting on a two-person play that he and his friend had written, and he was "discovered" by a famous actor named Spalding Gray. He was hired shortly after to be a part of an experimental theater group in the West Village called the Performing Garage. He went to school during the day and acted at night and on weekends. My mom, meanwhile, was making mocha chip pies for a nearby neighborhood restaurant. I am not sure how *she* got her gig, but all of this made me feel even more like we were essential residents.

I loved the inside of our apartment too. All our furniture was secondhand, colorful and mismatched, each piece with its own personality. The desk in my room was one that someone had left on the sidewalk, and we happily carried it the four blocks home. When my parents weren't off somewhere, they could both be found in our small kitchen cooking up something delicious or else listening to music or reading on our threadbare living room couch. On the second floor of our apartment, my brother and I had our bedrooms, bookended by a laundry room and a tiny TV room. There were lots of spaces for hide-and-seek. Music filled our home. Each of us had a record player and at any given time there was something on, someone dancing or singing badly with no shame. My father played the guitar and sometimes serenaded my mother with Rod Stewart songs because she was in love with Rod. She ended up co-owning an R&B/hip-hop/disco record label for a short period of time. As part of her "work," she took my father to clubs to hear DJs spin and to go dancing. I would jump and dance on her bed while Donna Summer played in the background as she dressed in her blue satin pants, flowy shirts, and Lucite heels and put on her makeup. She was beautiful and I am sure I got my clubbing gene from her.

At my West Village elementary school, we called our teachers by their first names and painted murals of our city on the walls of the playground courtyard. Michael and I walked home together each day, stopping at the deli for bagels or at the park to play on the swings with other neighborhood kids. Sometimes we would stop at the big public library branch close to home and Michael would help me pick out books like *The Phantom Tollbooth* or *Frog and Toad*, which he would read to me at night or we would discuss as if we had our own private book club. I am sure I got my love of reading from him. He always had a book in hand unless he was making mischief by dropping eggs or water balloons out of his window to the street below, until the therapist called our parents to complain. We often sat by his window watching the people below or across the way sitting on their fire escapes. In the evening when it was warm enough, we would sit out on our stoop together taking in the lit-up city. It was magical.

For middle school, my parents started sending me and Michael to a new school on the Upper East Side. They thought I would get a better education at this school, and it fit in with the lifestyle they were trying to cultivate as they plotted our family's eventual move uptown. At my new school, you absolutely could not be caught wearing the same thing every day, and whatever you did wear it must either have been designer or vintage but nothing in between unless you didn't want any friends at all. There went my suspenders. I rode the bus or the subway back and forth to school, depending on my mood. The bus gave me extra time to sleep or stare out the window before reaching home and having to think about homework. The subway was faster and much better for people watching. Commuting to and from school by myself made me feel like I could handle anything on my own.

Many of my new friends had huge apartments in doorman buildings that were so different from our downtown brownstone. No one had a stoop, with the exception of my two best friends, who lived much farther uptown in tiny walk-ups, with some stairs out front for chilling. But they *all* liked to hang out with me in the Village, and I also preferred the vibe of my neighborhood to the stiff and proper Upper East Side. There was a mystique and a feeling of rebellion to walking along West 8th Street in the evening, passing the punk rockers and the theater where *The Rocky Horror Picture Show* played. I took my new uptown friends to all my neighborhood spots, which made me feel interesting and powerful. We would sit on my Village stoop talking about crushes and smoking clove cigarettes, pretending our parents believed us when we told them we were carrying the packs "for a friend."

One night in eighth grade, I put on makeup and snuck out with a friend to go to Studio 54. Somehow, the velvet ropes were lifted for us, and we were let into this magical place to dance with celebrities and drag queens and all the beautiful people. We didn't drink or do any drugs, but we thought we were so grown up and nobody told us we didn't belong. The next morning, we sat on my stoop, drowsy from our adventure, thrilled that we hadn't gotten caught, and recapping the night between sips of coffee and puffs on a shared cigarette. I felt alive.

When I was in high school, we moved to the Upper West Side (slightly less rigid than the Upper East, but a far cry from the Village). My father was making more money by then and my parents had long aspired to be part of this well-heeled, uptown, doorman-building crowd. My brother Michael went off to college in LA, and eventually, he would graduate and make a new life for himself on the West Coast. He left me behind and I missed him terribly. Meanwhile, I felt like I'd had no say in my parents' decision to move. I craved my downtown life.

The move did little to hold my parents in one place. It didn't stop them from traveling and disappearing, but at this point in my teenage life, I longed for their absence and was happiest on my own. When they were around, I felt stifled and criticized, and the critical voices in my mind got louder and stronger. When my parents weren't there, it was easier to push those thoughts aside and hang on tight to my West Village girl. I filled the space with friends and parties so loud the neighbors called the police. I stayed out late, ate one-dollar pizza slices at four A.M., and savored my independence. I was as alive as the city around me. And whenever I felt like I was losing touch with my downtown girl, when words of worthlessness filled my brain, the Village was only a subway ride away. I could always find my way to a stoop to dream and make plans and feel like the real me.

Until I couldn't.

Until that was no longer enough.

The voices in my head became so loud, making me believe

that I was somehow broken. I became the girl defined by words like *annoying, anxious, ugly, weird, stupid, worthless.* Those would be the words I would use to create a new story of me. I forgot my worth, my power, myself. My little city girl faded. And I focused on the version of me that was full of flaws and in need of fixing.

When my own kids were little and their unique personalities began to emerge, I started to see, in each of them, the child on the outside who would someday become their inner child and suddenly my little West Village girl reemerged. She came out in full force. Like all of us before the words and the expectations of the world interfered, my children were full of wonder and freedom and self-love and courage. And *my* little downtown girl wanted to play. She wanted to love, to be strong and fierce and free right along with my kids. At first, I tried to keep her at bay. I was a mom, a grown-up, a big girl; what place did she have? But she stuck around and made herself heard. And when I finally decided to let her back in, I knew that I was home.

As I watch my kids grow into young adults, I think about the little kid versions of themselves still present inside. I think about the way that the world can sometimes feel like a mess. I know they hear unkind words, and I hear and see it when they are hard on themselves. And I wonder if their inner critics will drown the voices of their authentic, little kid selves—beautiful, and loving, and trying to speak their truth. Will my children struggle to remember who they are as I have? Or will this journey be smoother for them? Whatever happens, my hope is that they will find a way to take the hands of that child inside and never let go.

For all of the years that I had tried to silence and push away my own little downtown girl she was still there:

In the freedom of my club days

In the discovery of the practices of yoga and mindfulness

In the joy and fulfillment of teaching and writing

In the desire to make peace with my parents and myself

In the awe and newness of being a mom

In the wonder and playfulness of my children

She was there to forgive my mistakes. She was the one helping me to heal and to change the conversation with myself. She was filling my head and my heart with the thoughts and words that captured who I once was, who I still am. She is here. And I am holding onto her with all my might. Paying attention when she speaks. Letting her words drown out the words that have hurt me. She is that girl on the stoop formed by the city around her. That girl who was worthy all along.

I listen to my inner voice
telling me I am worthy.
Those words are my story.
They are the words that matter.

EPILOGUE:

FILLING
THE
SHELVES

Before our recent kitchen renovation, following the bathroom flood mentioned previously, we had a very cluttered pantry filled with snacks. It held other things too, but mostly it was the go-to location for all things "snacky." The pantry was strategically located at the bottom of a staircase that led directly to my kids' bedrooms on the second floor. When they or their friends emerged from their rooms seeking sustenance, all they had to do was run down the stairs and grab something off a shelf without needing to enter any other rooms and having to (God forbid) interact with other humans. My kids have always been grazers; sometimes their snacks are healthy and sometimes not so much, but I have learned not to get too concerned about their preferences. Once, when I was considering emptying the pantry of all the bags of popcorn and pretzels and nuts and goldfish and the rest and perhaps replacing them with other seemingly healthier options, one of Ben's friends said, "Susan, this is the best curated snack closet I have ever seen." This of course made me love the child for using the word "curated," and I decided to keep everything just as it was.

During the renovation, the pantry was relocated to the middle of the kitchen, which meant snack procurement required a bit more effort and a slight risk of crossing paths with an adult. But it was easily accessible, nonetheless. In the process of reorganizing, I found myself spending way too much time thinking about the snacks and how to "curate" them in this new space. How many shelves should be dedicated to these grab-and-go options? How could I make the snack pantry easy and appealing for the kids and their friends? Forget about putting dishes back on shelves or sorting the silverware drawers or even considering using that time for writing or meditation. NOPE! The snack pantry took priority.

The "kids," who are eighteen and seventeen, will be off to college soon and they are already living with one foot out the door. I really should be thinking about how to organize this new space for *me*. I really should be thinking about how to organize my *life* for me. They are living theirs and I have to figure out a new way to live mine as someone beyond mom. I will be the one here on my own, until holiday vacations bring us all back together—unless their new friends or significant others invite them elsewhere during those breaks. And how will I say no to that? I won't, because these are the experiences to be had and enjoyed. So why am I spending so much time on these snacks? Do I think that if the pantry is appealing enough, it will be the thing to tether them to home? Of course, I know how silly that sounds. But in this moment, the snacks are actually tethering *me* to them. Somehow filling the shelves with muscle milks and granola bars is a comfort, a task, something I can physically do to make me feel needed and necessary. My way of holding on.

Here I am again, back in this familiar place, with the next phase of life testing my practices. I find myself grasping for something I can control (snacks), in the face of things I have no control over. However, at this point in my journey, I know how to be curious and take a step back to ask myself "What's really going on?" The answer is, I am afraid. I am afraid of this big change. I am afraid that because I haven't figured out how to be a perfect parent, that because I have made mistakes and sometimes struggled, maybe I haven't given them enough of a solid foundation to face what is ahead. I am afraid of being alone and having to navigate my life as someone other than the mother I have been for eighteen years. Who will I be? Will the connection I have with my kids grow stronger, or will I become the occasional, obligatory phone call?

As each of these fears float into my mind, I accept them with compassion, and I breathe. I make a choice not to get on the crazy train of emotion that I have boarded so many times before. I tell myself, it's OK to be afraid. No, I don't know how the future will play out, but I don't have to. I do know how to be in this place of unknown. I can laugh at the ridiculousness of filling a pantry with snacks to keep my kids from growing up. I can also love this side of myself and how much I care, I worry, I try. I can think about the exciting possibilities that are ahead for all of us. I can recognize how lucky I am to love my kids so hard that I ache at even the thought of distance between us. And I know they feel lucky too.

I will probably keep putting snacks on the shelves for whenever the kids come home, mostly because it makes me feel connected. But I'll do it knowing the reasons and being conscious of my choice. And in this noticing, I'll find the loving words that I need to hear, the ones that have been inside of me all along. I will speak to myself with kindness and ground myself in the here and now.

In this moment
I reconnect to me.

In this moment
everything is all right.

In this moment
I am all right.

ACKNOWLEDGMENTS

The writing of this book has been a journey that I could not have taken without the help and support of many.

Thank you, thank you, Erica Rand Silverman of Stimola Literary Studio. You are agent extraordinaire, true friend, and believer in the power of books. When I mentioned wanting to write for adults, without hesitation you said, "Yes, let's do it!" and began to make it happen without skipping a beat. You always encourage me to be authentic and put forward work that I believe in and are there to rein me in when my mind spirals. Also, thank you for each of your read-alouds that make every manuscript feel like love.

Jessica Sindler, executive editor at Kevin Anderson & Associates, for your gentle way of making it easier to be vulnerable, go deeper, and be open to suggestion.

Rebecca Kaplan, editor in chief at Abrams Image, for also saying yes, and for your never waning interest, support, and kindness, letting this book become what it was meant to be and for indulging all of my overthinking.

Michael Sand, publisher at Abrams, whose input and thoughtfulness led to a beautiful title, and art director Diane Shaw, who visually brought the essence of this book to life.

Michael Jacobs, for believing in my choices and making me feel like I am part of a family of intentional and thoughtful creators looking to make the world a more interesting and loving place.

The team at Abrams Kids, for having my back and being champions of meaningful books for children.

My three beautiful, amazing children! Thank you for letting me share parts of your stories in order to tell mine, for encouraging me to keep going even when I wanted to give up and sit on the couch and binge watch *Below Deck* instead of working, and for letting me be your mom. You are my whole heart.

My own mama, for the walks and talks on and off the beach, and the openness and honesty and love we have found with each other that has brought us closer. You made it feel safer to share. You are beautiful inside and out.

My brother, Michael, for making me laugh even when it seemed impossible to find anything funny. I hope you know in your heart you are enough.

Rachael, for helping me see all sides and reminding me of what our dads would say in any given situation.

Marie-Caroline Caiola, for your endless love and friendship and constant reminders to let go of the outcome, get out of my own way, and tap into the ocean.

To my yoga teachers past and present, you have no idea how instrumental you are in making this and all of my creative endeavors happen. You help me find my breath when it seems to have left me.

My friends, who see me and love me and lift me.

Courtney Sheinmel, for your friendship, excitement, and encouragement, for critiquing with honesty and compassion, and for letting me know that feeling nauseated while writing meant I was on the right path.

Tony Morrison, you reappeared just in time to remind me that my city girl is still full of life. Thank you for sending me your house music mixes so good I had to walk away from the computer to dance.

Clara Garnica (aka mama #2), for helping me with everything else so I had enough brain space to create.

Gizmo, Oliver, and Dakota, you are the best distractions and full of oft-needed (albeit sometimes reluctant but always the best) snuggles.

Dad, miss you. Wish you were here for this and everything else.